TUNING & REPAIRING
YOUR OWN
PIANO

BY JIM JACKSON

TAB | **TAB BOOKS Inc.**
BLUE RIDGE SUMMIT, PA 17214

To Linda, who gave me the reasons I needed for doing this book.

FIRST EDITION

FIRST PRINTING

Library of Congress Cataloging in Publication Data

Jackson, Jim, 1947-
    Tuning and repairing your own piano.

    Includes index.
    1. Piano—Tuning.   2. Piano—Maintenance and repair.
I. Title.
MT165.J3   1984   786.2′3   83-24332
ISBN 0-8306-1678-0 (pbk.)

Contents

Preface

I wanted to write this book because I acquired my initial education in piano technology only from written material. In the process, I became painfully aware of the assumptions and gaps in information present in the books previously written on the subject. I have tried to make no assumptions about your previous education and have attempted to provide step-by-step directions that will allow you to proceed in an orderly manner in learning to tune and repair pianos. I have included all the basic information that is required so that you do not have to guess about the procedure to be followed.

I would like to thank Rich Strader for the time and expertise he provided in taking and preparing the photographs for this book, as well as for the technical advice and encouragement that he offered.

I would also like to thank Denny Hayes and House of Baldwin in Colorado Springs. The many hours of experimentation needed in preparation for this book were spent in his store on his fine instruments. He also allowed me the use of his facilities and pianos as models for all the photographs.

I believe a special thank-you should go to my parents, whose interests in the physical sciences and music led me into this interesting and rewarding field. Besides, they had to listen to my incessant pounding on my own piano while I was learning to tune.

Introduction

This book is written for the person who would like to learn tuning and repairing of pianos, either as a hobby or as a business to generate all or part of his income. Piano tuning, because it involves matching sounds, might seem impossible to learn from printed material alone. This is not the case. The biggest problem encountered in learning to tune a piano is training the ear to hear the correct sounds. Because sounds cannot be pointed to, the sounds the student needs to listen for must be described. A description is just as effective in print as in person.

A piano generates many kinds of sounds when it is played. Some of these sounds are not musical and can be classified only as noises. The student of piano tuning must learn to ignore these noises as well as many of the musical sounds the piano makes. The bulk of the ear training that allows the piano tuner to ignore irrelevant sounds comes from practice. Because the purpose of instruction is to describe the sounds of the piano, each individual must get the best descriptions he can and use them to learn to identify the sounds in question. Piano tuners use sounds that tend to pulsate. An instructor present when the student is practicing can help by visually indicating the speed of the pulsations. The individual working with a book as a guide can accomplish the same thing, although he may need a bit more patience and practice.

Repairing a piano, or any other mechanical device, involves learning how the mechanism works. Although having another person point to each part and show how it moves and interacts with other parts may make learning somewhat quicker, this type of instruction is easily forgotten and may have to be repeated several times. The student who learns by observing the operation of the piano while studying a written text is learning by experience, which is always the best teacher. It may take a bit longer to grasp the concepts, but once they are understood they will not be forgotten. Once the student has familiarized himself with the principles of the piano's operation, he will have the information needed to rectify most of the problems he will encounter when working on the instruments. At the very least, he will be able to intelligently discuss any problem with a more experienced technician if he finds a repair that he cannot make.

Background information on the history and construction of the piano is presented so that the student might understand how the instrument evolved to its present state. Unlike some instruments, the piano was not originally designed in its modern form. Instead, it evolved from other instruments and continued to change in order to meet the requirements of those who played it.

Although an extensive knowledge of the physics and mathematical theories of sound and music is not required, the tuner should have some understanding of what sound is and how it relates to music and scale development. This information is presented in a way that should not mire the student in unnecessary details, but should provide him with enough information to know why he tunes as he does.

Once sufficient background information has been presented, the book describes the actual processes used in tuning the piano. Emphasis is on practice exercises that should allow the student to progress as quickly as possible. Following these exercises should minimize the problems normally encountered when training the ear and when developing proper muscle coordination.

Tests to check the accuracy of the tuning are explained and should be used from the beginning. Professional tuners continue to use these tests on each piano they tune. The tests are not merely an aid to the novice, but an intrinsic part of the tuning process. The nature and use of these tests have been overlooked in many books and classes. I hope the student will be able to use them to develop good tuning skills without the benefit of personal instruction.

Another feature, which I believe is unique, has been added to the description of the tuning process. This feature involves describing the pitch of the sound the student should listen for when tuning each note. Because the piano produces many different sounds when played, the beginner often has difficulty determining just which sound should be used for the tuning. The correct sound is identified by giving a reference note on the keyboard. This note, when played on the piano keyboard, should produce a tone that is close to the pitch of the sound he should listen for.

A piano tuner cannot merely concern himself with the process of tuning. The workings of both the grand and vertical piano is discussed. The most common types of repairs, as well as the proper adjusting of the various moving parts, are explained.

In the last chapter considerable attention is given to the business aspects of piano tuning and repairing. Many technicians, although highly qualified, have difficulty making a living at their craft because they have not considered their work as a business. Unless an individual wants to learn piano tuning only as a hobby, these business skills must be learned. Little attention has been paid to these business skills in previous books. The aim of any technical training is normally to enable the student to develop skills that he can use to produce income. If you intend to use piano technology to supplement your income, or as your full-time vocation, the information presented should aid you in effectively generating this income.

Throughout this book, I have assumed that you have no previous knowledge of music or the piano. Some of the information presented may be unnecessary to some people. Many, for example, will not need the explanation of musical notation. It is logical to assume that many who wish to learn piano tuning have some background in piano and can read music. It is just as logical to assume that many do not. Some very talented and successful pianists cannot read music, so there is no reason to assume that talented and highly trained piano technicians knew how to read music before their training began. Because I needed a way to tell which notes were being discussed, musical notation was introduced for those unfamiliar with it. If this or other background information seems unnecessary, keep in mind it is presented so that no one will be excluded from using this book to learn piano technology, regardless of previous education.

Chapter 1

Piano Facts

Piano tuning is a largely misunderstood art that can be an exciting hobby or a rewarding profession. Many people think that a piano tuner must be an accomplished pianist with perfect pitch. Most people think he tunes by remembering how a musical scale should sound and by adjusting the piano to match his memory. These are misconceptions.

A piano tuner is an ordinary man or woman who has invested a relatively small amount of money in tools and a rather large amount of time and patience in learning to hear and adjust some special sounds the piano makes. Piano tuning can be learned by anyone who has good hearing and concentration. The length of time required depends on the individual and on the amount of time he has to devote to the practice exercises. The average person could probably learn to do an acceptable tuning in six months to a year, provided he has a few hours a day for practice.

Piano tuning has some peculiarities that make it especially advantageous as a profession for certain groups of people. Because piano tuning does not require great physical strength, it offers a good opportunity for women and people with physical handicaps. Because women tend to have better hearing and better manual dexterity than men, they have a definite advantage. It is also a good opportunity for women because those new to the trade are generally well accepted by those who are already technicians. Acceptance is based more on ability and attitude than on any preconceived notions about either sex.

The opportunity in piano tuning for the blind has long been recognized, but it is also a good job for people whose physical disabilities keep them from doing heavy physical work. If one is tall enough, he can tune a piano while sitting. By being an independent businessman, the handicapped person can arrange his work around any problems his disability might cause. Also, his ability to support himself is based on his determination, craftsmanship, and business practices. Success does not depend upon how an employer might judge his abilities or disabilities.

When learning to tune a piano accurately, one must first train the ear to hear *harmonics*. When a piano wire vibrates to produce a sound, it also emits a whole series of tones called harmonics. These auxiliary sounds are much quieter and higher in pitch than the basic tone one recognizes as a note in the musical scale. The piano tuner learns to isolate these sounds and compare the harmonics of one note with those of another. They are used as guideposts so that the tuner is not left to use only his memory of a musical scale when adjusting the pitch of the piano. Once one has learned to recognize and use these guideposts, finding the proper pitch for a note is not much more difficult than driving from one city to another using a good map as a guide. Learning to tune a piano is largely a matter of learning to read an audible map.

DEVELOPMENT OF MUSIC AND MUSICAL INSTRUMENTS

From his earliest beginnings, man has surrounded himself with music. Prehistoric man was faced with a chaotic world full of harsh and frightening noises. He soon found that he could make sounds of a more pleasing nature. These seemed to soothe him and temper the harsher noises of his environment. His simplest instrument was his voice. With it, he could communicate with other men, warn of dangers, and lull his children to sleep. He discovered later that he could augment his singing with a variety of instruments. The simplest may have involved beating on a hollow log and plucking the string of his hunting bow. These early discoveries, that pleasant sounds could be produced by plucking one object or striking another, would eventually lead to the development of the piano.

In time, early man found that he could make musical tones by blowing across the end of a reed. He varied the tone by blowing harder or by changing the pressure of his lips as he blew across the reed. With experimentation he found he could change the pitch of the sound by changing the length of the reed and by cutting holes along its length that could be covered and uncovered by his fingers. This led to the development of the *Pan's Pipe*, which was quite possibly the earliest musical instrument capable of producing a series of tones at different pitches.

Experimentation and development of musical instruments continued, and music found its way into the Greek culture. The Greeks, who are credited with beginning Western musical culture, introduced music into religious and social gatherings. Pythagoras, who lived about 500 B.C., began the first experiments on the relationships of various musical tones. These experiments eventually led to the development of scales. They also led to organized, structured music that could be recorded in written form so that it could be reproduced by any group of musicians at any time. During the time of the Greeks the simple Pan's Pipe developed into the organ.

Until the advent of the organ, each Pan's Pipe had a narrow range of tones that it could produce. In order to get much higher or lower tones, pipes of different lengths were used. It took a group of musicians with pipes of different lengths to produce reasonably complex music covering the entire range of pleasant tones. All of these tones could be produced by one musician if the pipes were all fastened together, along with an air pump that would blow across all of them at once. The earliest organs were that simple, and the pipes that were not to produce a sound had to be closed off by the musician's hands. Eventually mechanical devices were used to close off the unwanted pipes. The keyboard was the musician's means for opening and closing the desired pipes.

While the reed instruments were developing into the organ, stringed instruments were also evolving. For centuries, the harp was the principal stringed instrument being used. In order to make more complicated forms of music possible, a mechanical device that could connect the player to the strings was desired. This would decrease the difficulty encountered when plucking the strings with fingers. Mallets, similar to those used with percussion instruments, were the simplest device available. Combining mallets with stringed instruments led to piano precursors such as the hammer dulcimer.

Borrowing from the keyboard concept of the organ, musicians made an important step in the development of the percussive stringed instruments with the *clavichord*. The clavichord has an extremely simple mechanism. It has keys, like those found on the

3

modern piano. At the inner end of the key is a knife edge called the *tangent*. It is similar to the point of a chisel. When the key is depressed, the tangent rises to strike a string. After hitting the string, the tangent is held against it by keeping the key depressed. By so doing, the tangent also becomes a bridge, which determines the pitch of the note. By varying the pressure on the key, the string tension can be slightly increased and decreased, adding a *vibrato*, a tremulous effect, if desired. The clavichord's simple design makes it a very delicate sounding instrument. Its main drawback is that it is very quiet. It is so quiet that it is hard to hear a clavichord being played in a room where normal conversation is being carried on.

The next stage in the attempt to insert a mechanism between the musician and the strings was the *harpsichord*. The working mechanism of the harpsichord is slightly more complex than the clavichord's, but much simpler than the modern piano's. At the inner end of a harpsichord key is a vertical piece called the *jack*. Attached to the jack is a *plectrum*, which was originally made of quill. The plectrum plucks the string as the jack rises. It then travels past the string, which is allowed to vibrate freely. The plectrum is hinged to the jack in such a way that it can swivel and slide down past the string when the key is released. This movement keeps the string from being plucked a second time when the jack moves back to its rest position.

The harpsichord was a major improvement over the clavichord because it produced a sound loud enough to be heard when combined with other stringed instruments in a chamber group. It is, however, still a very quiet instrument. Because the strings of a harpsichord are plucked, they must be of a relatively light gauge, so the sound it produces is still too quiet to be heard when played with a full concert orchestra. The search continued for a percussive stringed instrument that had a larger dynamic range, one that could play loudly as well as softly.

DEVELOPMENT OF PIANOS AND PIANO TUNING

The first instrument that can be called a piano was built about 1710 by an Italian named Bartolomeo Christofori. In order to get more volume, he replaced the plectrum and jack of the harpsichord with a knob hammer that struck the string. Even though the mechanism used by Christofori was simple compared to the modern piano's, his instrument was capable of producing both loud and soft sounds. He called it a *piano-forte*. Piano means soft, and forte means loud. Eventually, the instruments that evolved from Christofori's simple instrument became known simply as the piano.

Many improvements were later made on the first pianos. In the early piano-fortes the strings were struck by the hammer and allowed to vibrate undamped, until the sound finally died away. The invention of the sustain pedal allowed the string to sound only so long as the musician wished. A soft pedal, which made it possible to play softer sounds more easily, was also introduced. The soft pedal gave the piano more dynamic range in quiet sounds. To increase the dynamic range further, improvements were made that allowed the piano to play louder than the early models. This was done by using heavier wire strung at higher tensions. The modern piano wire may have 150-200 pounds of tension upon it. Because a modern grand piano may have about 250 wires, the total tension supported by the frame of the piano approaches 40,000 pounds.

A stringed instrument, whether a piano or a violin, has its strings fastened securely at one end. The other end of each string is wound around a peg. Turning the peg changes the tension of the string and, therefore, its pitch. The pegs of the violin and guitar are contained in a box attached by gears to a key that is used to turn them. The key is part of the instruments. The harp, clavichord, and harpsichord have *tuning pins*. A tuning pin is a peg imbedded in wood. A key is fit onto the end of the pin in order to turn it. These instruments, which have relatively low string tensions compared to the piano, must be tuned frequently. When harpsichords were the predominant keyboard instruments, the musician tuned his instrument before each concert, just as a harp player does today.

As the piano evolved, higher string tension meant that the tuning pins must be held very tightly in the wood block. Otherwise, the pin would unwind, and the instrument would go out of tune very quickly. This meant that great force must be exerted to overcome the grip of the wood against the tuning pin. At the same time, the pin only needed to be turned by very small amounts to change the pitch drastically. The key used for tuning harps and clavichords was replaced by a tool that provides more leverage. Special skills were needed to use this tool effectively, so musicians were no longer able to tune their own instruments.

At the same time that the harpsichord and piano were being developed, changes were taking place in the nature of the musical scale being used. These changes placed a greater importance on how the keyboard instruments were tuned. There was much less room for error with the new way the scale was being tuned. These changes, along with the physical complexities of tuning the piano because of its high tensions, led to the birth of piano tuning as a profession.

As the art of tuning grew with the development of the piano, the piano tuner became an artist in his own right. Becoming a concert quality tuner requires as much time and skill as becoming a concert quality pianist does. The musician practices his craft on stage in front of an audience. The tuner, who practices his art in privacy, is also a performer. If he does poorly, the quality of the musician's performance is affected. The piano tuner is indeed a special kind of musician. Without him, we would not have the quantity or quality of piano music that we do.

Working on pianos has two aspects. One is tuning, which involves putting all of the notes of the piano at the correct pitch. The other is the repairing and adjusting of the mechanism of the instrument. This aspect is more appropriately called piano technology and is done by a piano technician. Since all tuners of notes can also do repairs and adjustments, the term *tuner-technician* has become popular. In this book, the terms tuner, technician, and tuner-technician will be used interchangeably to describe that individual who tunes and repairs or adjusts the various parts of the piano.

PIANO CONSTRUCTION

Because most of the pianos most tuners work on are of the *vertical* type, this discussion of piano construction will be concerned only with this type of design. Vertical pianos are so called because the plane of the strings is vertical. In *grand pianos,* the plane of the strings is horizontal, but the principles of construction are the same.

Vertical pianos can be divided into several groups. One group is the large old type called the *upright piano.* Because of their size, they have fallen into disfavor during the past 20 to 30 years and have been replaced by *spinet* or *console* pianos. The difference between a spinet and console is basically in height and to some extent in the placement of the piano's mechanical parts in relation to the keys. These smaller pianos fit much better into the small rooms of modern homes and so have become very popular. They generally stand 36"-45" high. Some of the case parts are a bit different in design from the upright's, but once one is familiar with the older piano, the names of the various case parts can be accurately transferred to the smaller piano, even though they may vary in appearance.

To understand the design of the piano, six basic components can be considered. These are the case, the tuning pins, the soundboard and bridges, the pinblock and tuning pins, the strings, and the keys and action.

The Case

The *case* of the piano consists of all the visible wood parts that enclose the instrument. While they may vary somewhat in shape or design from one piano to the next, they serve the same function, and can be named and identified. Figure 1-1 shows the names of the case parts of a typical upright piano. One part of the case that is not so readily visible, but which must be considered, is the supporting members, which may be seen from the back of the piano. These usually consist of five 4″ × 4″ vertical supports placed between two horizontal supports that run the width of the piano.

In order to see the inside of the piano, some of the case parts must be removed. Usually it is not necessary to move the piano from a wall in order to do this. The first step in disassembling the case is to open the *lid*. It will be hinged at the back, the front being held in place with spring clips, so it is only necessary to lift up on the front of the lid. Some old pianos have one long hinge, running the width of the piano, placed in the middle of the lid (front to back). With this arrangement, the front part of the lid lifts up and folds back over the rear portion.

Before opening the lid of any piano, it is wise to check to see that the hinge pins are still in place, so that the lid can be opened safely. This is especially important on old pianos located in restaurants and lounges because the pins may have been deliberately removed so that the top could be taken off easily in order to make the piano sound louder.

Once the lid has been propped open, it is necessary to remove the front panel. On spinets and consoles, the front panel may be combined with the music shelf and music rack. This all comes off as one unit. It may simply lift off, or may be held in place with screws or catches at either end.

On uprights, the front panel may be hung on the pilasters. With this design, the front is lifted off, although it may also have catches at either end. On some uprights, the front panel and pilasters come off as a unit. If the front panel comes off alone, the pilasters will have to be removed before the case can be disassembled further. They are usually screwed into the sides of the piano. Once the pilasters are removed, the screws that hold the music shelf in place will be exposed. After removing the music shelf, close the name board, and the screws that hold it will be found at each end of the strip of wood

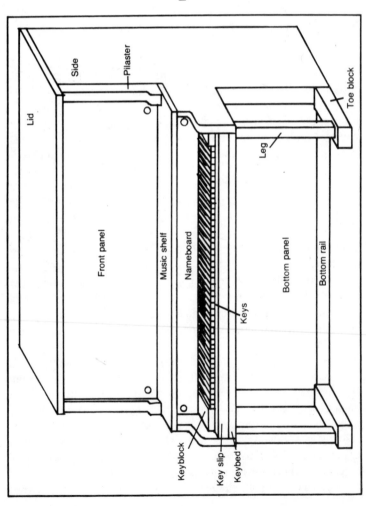

Fig. 1-1. Upright piano case.

8

to which it is hinged. Case designs vary, but a few minutes of inspection and a little common sense will show the piano tuner how to take the case apart.

The Plate

The *plate,* also called the *casting* or *harp,* is the cast-iron frame upon which the piano wires are strung. Cast iron is needed to support the tremendous stresses in the piano. The plate is an integral part of the piano and should not be ignored by the tuner.

Before tuning an old piano, it is a good idea to check for cracks that may have started in the cast iron. The bolts that secure the plate to the frame of the piano should also be checked to make sure they are tight. Any loose bolts should be tightened. Because of the amount of stress on it, the plate has the potential to become a dangerous object if it should break or come loose from the frame. Cracks that have started may worsen with the tuning. As a result, the piano will not stay in tune. If the tuner tries to raise the pitch too far, the increased tension may cause the plate to break, thereby totally ruining the instrument. Except on very fine, expensive pianos, it is generally too costly a proposition to repair a broken harp.

One part of the plate worth noting is the small hooked protrusions near the bottom, which the strings are hooked onto or looped around. These are the *hitch pins*, and their purpose is to secure the bottom end of the piano wires.

Soundboard and Bridges

The *soundboard* of the piano is responsible for amplifying the sound made by the vibrating piano wire. The soundboard is a thin piece of wood, commonly spruce, of large area. The purpose of the *bridge* is to provide a fixed end point for that portion of the wire that is free to vibrate, as well as to transmit the vibration to the soundboard.

In practice, the bridges rest upon the soundboard, and the strings press down upon the bridges. When a string is set into motion, the vibrations are transmitted through the bridge to the soundboard, causing its entire area to vibrate. This makes the sound loud enough to be easily heard. Even though it is more difficult to make wood begin vibrating, it is used in place of other material because it affects the quality of the sound produced. Wood makes a much richer sound than other materials.

The bridges, which are fastened to the soundboard, have a

series of pins inserted into them. The strings pass by these staggered bridge pins, which hold the strings at fixed points along the bridge. It should be noted that the strings are farther from the soundboard at the bridge than at either end (Fig. 1-2). This causes a

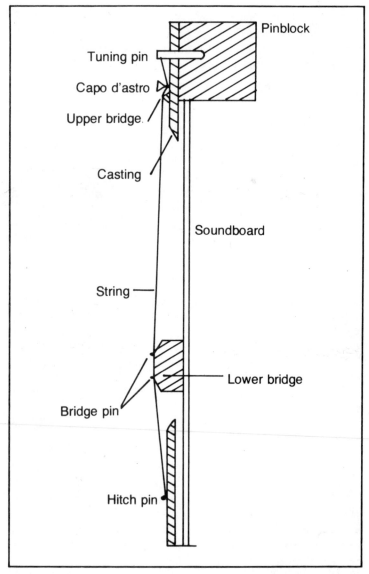

Fig. 1-2. Cross sectional representation of piano construction (front of piano to left).

bowed configuration that makes the strings push down upon the bridge and soundboard. This downbearing is important in making sure the sound is effectively transmitted to the soundboard.

Pinblock and Tuning Pins

The *pinblock* is a plank of hard wood as wide as the piano; it is found near the top of the instrument. It is actually made of several layers of hardwood, usually maple. The grain of each layer runs in a different direction from the grain of adjacent layers. The pinblock may not be visible if the top of the casting is designed to cover it. In such a case, there will be a hole in the casting where each *tuning pin* is inserted.

The tuning pins are steel, which has been blued or nickle plated to prevent rusting. One end of the piano wire will be wound around the tuning pin and inserted through a small hole. Depending on the design of the piano, there will be between 230 and 250 tuning pins. By turning the pin, tension on the wire can be increased or decreased. Increasing the tension causes the vibrating wire to produce a higher pitch. Decreasing tension lowers pitch.

Although the tuning pins do have a very fine thread on the end that is inserted into the pinblock, they are not screwed into it. They are driven into holes that have been drilled in the wood and are held in place only by the friction of the wood fibers against the tuning pin. As a piano gets older and the wood dries out, the cells in the wood contract, causing the tuning pin holes to enlarge. This may make the pins very loose, and such a piano will not hold a tune for long. Sometimes the pins can become so loose the piano cannot be tuned at all. Even though not all old pianos suffer from loose tuning pins, it is something to be aware of.

Strings

The *strings* are responsible for producing sound in the piano. A string is fastened to a tuning pin at one end, and the casting at the other. A section of the string is free to vibrate. That section begins at the wooden bridge near the bottom of the string. The vibrating section ends toward the top of the string when it passes over a bridge made of wood or a metal bridge that is part of the casting.

Instead of bridges, the piano may have *agraffes* at the tops of the strings. Agraffes are metal tabs with holes in them. A string passes through the hole and then goes on to be fastened to the tuning pin. An agraffe is really a separate bridge for each set of strings that make up one note.

If the string passes over a metal bridge at its upper end, it will then pass under a bar called the *capo d'astro*. This bar presses down on the string. The purpose of the bridge/capo arrangement, and of the agraffe also, is to hold the string in a fixed position and to provide a fixed end point for the vibrating portion of the string.

The piano has two different types of strings. These are the *wound strings* and *unwound strings*. Wound strings are found primarily in the bass, although they may be found in the tenor section of smaller pianos. They are made by wrapping a heavy metal winding around a core wire. Quality instruments have windings made of copper although some pianos may have strings wound with steel or steel coated with copper.

The purpose of the winding is to make the string heavier. A wire can be made to produce a lower pitch when it vibrates by making it either heavier or longer or by decreasing the tension on it. The tension on the wires must remain within certain limits in order for the piano to perform properly, so piano designers are left with changing either length or weight. Without the extra weight the winding provides, bass strings would have to be prohibitively long. The winding is only on that part of the string that is free to vibrate. Only the core wire passes over the bridges. Each wound string has a loop at the bottom, which is fastened to a hitch pin.

The strings in the tenor and treble sections of the piano are made of unwound steel wire. It will appear that there are three strings for each note in this part of the piano whereas there are only one or two in the bass. Closer inspection will show that what appears to be two strings in the tenor and treble is actually one piece of wire, even though the two halves may belong to different notes and have different pitches when the piano is tuned. The friction of the string against the bridge pins keeps the two halves from slipping and allows each to maintain a separate pitch. Figure 1-3 shows a representation of this aspect of piano design.

Keys and Action

The *keys* and *action* of a piano are what differentiate it from other modern stringed instruments such as violins and basses. These instruments require that the musician not only be able to excite the string properly, but that he learn where to place his fingers along the string in order to produce the correct pitch. In the piano, there is a separate set of strings for each note in the musical scale and a corresponding key for each set of strings. Pressing down on a given key operates a series of levers. These levers activate a

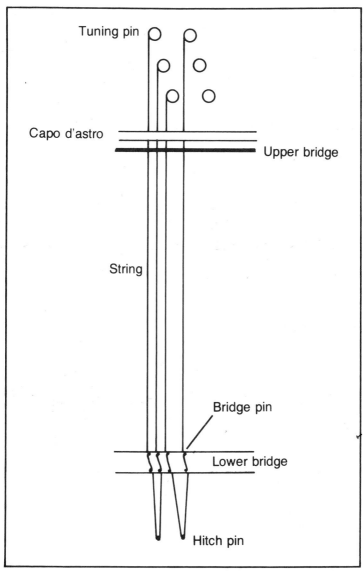

Fig. 1-3. Front view of treble stringing design.

hammer, which is made of dense felt, causing it to strike the strings. No matter how one pushes or hits the key, the pitch of the sound produced will always be the same. The use of the hammer eliminates the necessity of the musician to use his hands to produce the correct pitch. Producing the right pitch has become the job of the piano tuner and is accomplished before the music is actually to be played.

Again considering violins and basses, a string is set into motion by drawing a bow of horse hair across it. The pressure of the bow against the string, and its motion, drastically affects the quality of the sound the string emits. In the piano, the hammer will always hit the string in the same manner, no matter how the musician strikes the key. The sound quality, called the *timbre,* will therefore always be the same, so the musician can only alter the volume and duration of the tone. Changing the timbre is done by changing the density or hardness of the felt on the hammer. Varying the timbre is called *voicing,* and it is also the job of the piano tuner.

The mechanism of levers, springs, and wires that is interposed between the key and the hammer is called, collectively, the action. The design and operation of the upright and grand actions will be covered in detail later.

WHY THE PIANO GOES OUT OF TUNE

Many of the components of the piano are very elastic. The strings are in actuality a very high-grade stainless steel wire, which must be very elastic in order to vibrate properly and produce the desired tone. The thin spruce of the soundboard, when properly constructed, becomes like a very elastic spring. The more elastic it is, the better the tone coming from it. The wood of the pinblock, although it is very dense and not actually elastic, is subject to changes due to expansion and contraction of the wood cells. All of these components are subject to the high stresses the strings create in the instrument. These stresses have been seen to be between 18 and 20 tons.

This construction makes the piano very sensitive to changes in the weather. When the piano is exposed to increased humidity, the wood of the soundboard and bridges readily absorbs the moisture. This causes them to swell, which stretches the strings tighter, increasing their pitch. When the weather becomes drier, the moisture leaves the wood and the parts shrink. In many parts of this country, pianos are exposed to excessive humidity during the spring and summer. When houses are heated during the winter, the air becomes very dry. These drastic changes cause the string tensions and, therefore, the pitch to fluctuate. Even in more constant climates, these processes are constantly going on, although to a lesser degree.

In addition to moisture, temperature also has an effect on the piano. It causes the wood, the steel of the strings, and the cast-iron plate to expand and contract. Even barometric changes have an effect on tuning stability, although to a lesser degree.

In addition to dimensional changes in the piano's parts, the way the tuning pins are held in place must be considered. These pins are held only by the friction of wood fibers against metal. The tension of the strings is constantly trying to unwind the pin. This movement would reduce its tension and drop the pitch. Every change in the dimensions of the wood cells in the pinblock causes a change in the amount of grip they have on the tuning pins, giving them an opportunity to slip slightly. Whether these changes are due to moisture or temperature, the net result is the same, and the piano will drop a bit in pitch.

Another factor in tuning stability is the nature of the piano wire itself. Nothing remains elastic indefinitely, and the wire is no exception. After the piano is strung, there is a continuing tendency for the wire to lose its elasticity. In other words, the stress on the wire causes it to relax. When the string stretches this way, its tension and pitch are lowered.

This relaxing process is most notable in the first year or two after a piano has been built or completely restrung. It slows as the piano gets older. As a result, a new piano needs to be tuned more often than one that is several years old. A new piano should be tuned three or four times in the first year or two after it is built. This conflicts with what many people think will happen. They think that their new piano will be like their new car and that it will need less attention at first than it will later. As a result, many new pianos are left unattended for several years. When they finally are tuned, it becomes a more complicated and expensive proposition because the overall pitch of the instrument has dropped drastically.

Note that all of these factors affecting tuning stability do not depend on whether the piano is played. If it has been properly tuned, casual playing in the home will have less effect on the tuning than the drastic weather changes that are encountered in some parts of the country. Heavy use and hard playing will affect the tuning more than normal home use.

Fortunately, the effects of all these changes that take place in the piano tend to have a small effect on the accuracy of the tuning over the short run. While it might be said that no piano can stand in tune for more than 24 hours, it stays close enough that it will still sound pleasant. Unless the piano is played very hard for several hours each day, a proper tuning will still sound quite good after several weeks. It should sound good even after several months, providing there have been no drastic environmental changes.

After the first year or two of a piano's life, two tunings each year should be sufficient to keep it sounding good. A piano should be tuned at least once each year. Otherwise, its pitch may fall drastically overall, even though it may sound fairly well in tune with itself. A drop in pitch of one-half step, meaning C sharp has the pitch C should have, causes a drop in the total tension on the piano of approximately 5,000 pounds. If a piano is allowed to fall this far between tunings, the extreme change in tension resulting from tuning it back to the correct pitch can have only a detrimental effect on the instrument and shorten its useful life.

Chapter 2

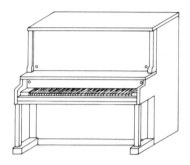

The Nature of Sound

Sound can be defined in two ways. The first definition considers only the physical phenomenon and states that sound is the vibration of a solid, liquid, or gas. The other definition has a more philosophical nature. It does not deny the existence of the physical vibrations, but insists that an ear must be present to sense them and transmit this information to the brain where it is perceived as the sensation of sound. Both definitions are correct, depending on the context in which they are used. For the purposes of describing sound in such a way that it can be studied, the former definition is the one being considered.

Sounds may be perceived as either musical in nature or as noises, depending somewhat on the point of view of the listener. Noises tend to be irregular and often harsh, as with the sounds produced by automobile traffic or machinery. Musical sounds, like those produced by musical instruments or songbirds, tend to be more regular and pleasing to the ear. The concept of music then is a matter of perception rather than a matter of physics. The laws of physics do apply, however, to musical sounds.

A general knowledge of how these laws apply to music and the piano is necessary if the student is to understand why he tunes in the way he does and what he should listen for when practicing.

HOW SOUND TRAVELS

Since sound is defined as the vibration of a solid, liquid, or gas, it is obvious that it cannot occur until some object begins to vibrate. A simple demonstration of this can be done by striking a tuning fork so that it begins to produce its sound. By touching the tines very lightly, one can feel their vibrations. These vibrations of the tuning fork excite the air around it. The molecules of air that begin vibrating because of their proximity to the tuning fork transmit their energy to adjacent air molecules. This energy is transmitted from molecule to molecule until it reaches the ear of the listener.

An experiment that shows that transmission of sound is dependent on air can be done with an electric bell, a vacuum pump, and a bell jar. The electric bell is placed on a pad of soft cloth or foam rubber. This is to prevent the sounds of the bell from traveling through the plate, since solids transmit sound. The jar is then inverted over the bell, the vacuum pump turned on, and the air slowly evacuated. As the air is removed, the sound of the bell can be heard to become softer and softer. At some point, when the air becomes rarefied enough, the sound will die away completely, even though the clapper of the bell may still be seen working. Upon slowly returning the air to the chamber, the sound of the ringing bell will get increasingly louder.

Once it is clear that air is the medium that carries the vibrations of the sound's source to the ear, the question becomes how this happens. The answer is that sound moves in waves. To illustrate wave motion, imagine a pond when a rock is tossed into it. When the rock breaks the water's surface, waves form that appear to move toward the edge of the pond. This type of wave motion (Fig. 2-1) has certain properties that can be described and measured.

The places where the wave has the same height as the undisturbed water previously did are called *nodes* and are located at points A, B, C, and D. The *crests* and *troughs*, which are located at E, F, and G, are called *anti-nodes*. The height of a crest or depth of a trough, measured at the point where the wave is farthest from the original water line, is the *amplitude* of the wave. Another term which is used to describe waves is *cycle*. A cycle can be defined as a sequence of changing states that upon completion returns to a state that is identical to the original one.

Consider the wave shown in Fig. 2-1. The form of the wave changes from point A, where the rock hit the water, until it reaches point C. From point C on, the wave is repeating the form taken from A to C. In Fig. 2-1, A to C is one cycle. If the wave is considered to begin at point E, the waveform can be seen to begin repeating itself at point G, so E to G is also one cycle.

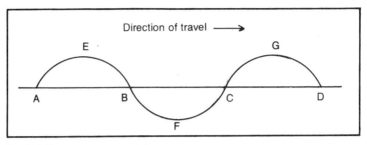

Fig. 2-1. Transverse wave motion.

Although the waveform appears to be moving away from the place where the rock hit the water, the actual particles of water are not moving laterally. If they did, the water would all pile up at the edge of the pond, and this is obviously not the case. The individual particles of water are instead moving up and down. Since the particles that make up the wave move across the path of the waveform, this is called a *transverse* wave. Although sound also travels in a wave, it takes a different form from that of the water.

To understand the sound wave, consider again the vibrating tuning fork. As a tine swings to the right, the air molecules along that side are pushed together. When the tine moves back to the left, a slight vacuum is created along its right side. This vacuum pulls on the particles of air that are closest to the tine, causing them to be spaced farther apart. When the tine moves once more to the right, the air molecules that were just pulled apart are pushed together again. As long as the tine continues to vibrate, the air particles will be repeatedly compressed and rarefied. This cyclic pattern of the molecules next to the fork is passed on to the other molecules that are near. The compression and rarefaction continue from one group of molecules to the next, with each particle being pushed and pulled from side to side.

The result is the type of wave shown in Fig. 2-2, where each vertical line represents the location of one molecule of air. One group of molecules is compressed while the one next to it is rarefied. This moving compression and rarefaction type of wave is called a *longitudinal* wave.

Even though the longitudinal wave has a different form from the transverse wave, the same terms are used to describe it. The crest of a longitudinal wave is that point where the particles are most compressed. The trough is the point of greatest rarefaction. In Fig. 2-2, the crests and troughs, still called anti-nodes, are located at E, F, and G. The nodes, at A, B, C, and D, are the points where

19

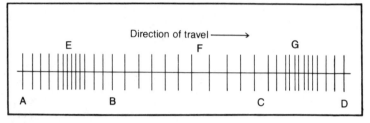

Fig. 2-2. Longitudinal wave motion.

the spacing of the air molecules is the same as it was before the air was disturbed. The amplitude of the anti-nodes refers to the amount or severity of the compressions and rarefactions. Because the longitudinal wave also repeats its form periodically, each repetition of form is still called one cycle.

The sensory characteristics of a sound that is heard by the ear can be measured and described by terms that apply to the waveform. As far as music is concerned, the three parameters used to describe the nature of sound are loudness, pitch, and timbre.

The loudness of a sound is related to the amplitude of its wave's anti-nodes. When a piano string is struck, it begins to vibrate in a complex manner, part of which takes the shape of a transverse wave. The amplitude of the string's vibrations is greater when the key is struck harder. The amplitude is a measure of the energy of the vibrations. The more energetic it is, the louder the sound will be.

Pitch refers to the perception of the sound's highness or lowness. When describing the physical characteristics of the wave that affect the pitch of a sound, the term *frequency* is used. Frequency is a measure of how often the waveform repeats itself, in other words, how often it cycles. The unit of time for such measurements is the second, so frequency is expressed in terms of the number of cycles that occur in one second. The abbreviation *cps* is used to indicate the number of *cycles per second*, hence, the frequency, of a sound. The higher the frequency and apparent pitch of a sound, the more cps it has.

Timbre is the term used to describe the quality of a sound. Timbre is what allows the listener to determine whether a sound was produced by a piano or a violin. Differences in timbre are a result of physical differences in the form the sound wave takes. When a piano string is struck, it vibrates in many different parts at the same time. Each vibrating segment produces a tone of a different frequency. These sounds are referred to as *harmonics, over-*

tones, or *partials*. Any vibrating body, not just a piano string, produces harmonics. The relative strength and pitch of the harmonics produced by different musical instruments produces the differences in waveform that create the timbre of each.

Because each sound produces a wave, consider what happens when two sounds are produced at the same time. Figure 2-3 shows two sound waves doing just this. Notice that the wave is shown in the transverse form, even though sound moving through air takes the form of a longitudinal wave. This representation is used because the transverse form is easier to draw and analyze.

The term *phase* is used to describe the relationships of the nodes and anti-nodes of two waves traveling simultaneously; Fig. 2-3 shows the situation where both sound waves have their crests and troughs occurring at the same time. These two waves are said to be *in phase*. Sound waves are *out of phase* if their crests and troughs occur at different times. The most extreme example of this is shown in Fig. 2-4, where the crest of one wave occurs while the other is in a trough.

When two sound waves are traveling at the same time, the amplitudes of each are added together to determine the volume the two produce together. To do this, positive and negative values need to be assigned to different portions of the wave. Any portion above equilibrium is assigned a positive value. Any part of the wave below

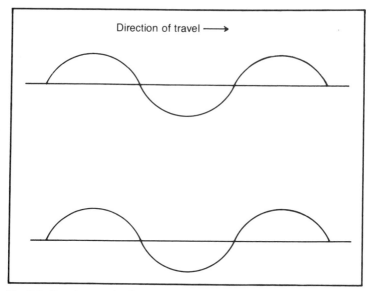

Fig. 2-3. Sound waves in phase.

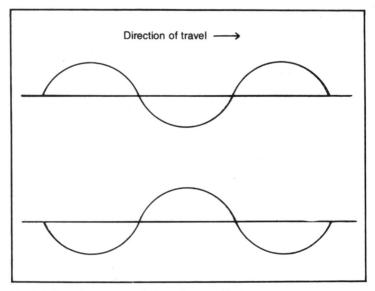

Fig. 2-4. Sound waves out of phase (in opposition).

equilibrium is given a negative value. Consider again Fig. 2-3. Both waves have their crests and troughs at the same time. If the amplitudes of each are the same, they are added together and the sum is twice that of either of the individual waves. This means that the waves enhance each other at all times, making the resulting sound twice as loud as either heard separately.

In Fig. 2-4, the crest of one wave is equal to, but in opposite phase, to the other. In this case, when the amplitudes of the two waves are added together, the positive crests are canceled out by the negative troughs. This would theoretically result in no sound being heard at all.

What happens though when two waves are only slightly out of phase as shown in Fig. 2-5? If one wave has a frequency of 440 cps and the other has a frequency of 441 cps, they are said to be 1 cps out of phase. To the human ear, this will result in a pulsating or warbling sound. These pulsations are called *beats* by piano tuners.

Beats are what the tuner uses to do his job correctly. He counts the number of beats that occur in one second. Sound waves that are 1 cps out of phase will produce a sound that beats once each second. If the waves are 2 cps out of phase, the sound will beat two times per second, and so on. Piano tuners do accurate work by learning to hear and count the beats that occur when two strings are sounding at the same time.

LAWS OF STRINGS

The frequency of the sound that a piano string produces when vibrating is governed by three laws of physics. These pertain to the length of the string, the tension on it, and its mass.

The First Law

Suppose that a piano string is struck and is vibrating at 440 cps. If the length of the string is effectively shortened by one-half, by placing a bridge at its mid-point, it will then vibrate at 880 cps, twice as fast as before. The same string will vibrate three times as fast, or 1320 cps, if it is shortened to one-third of its original length. As its length is shortened, the frequency of a vibrating string increases. This is called an *inverse proportion*. The frequency of a vibrating string is inversely proportional to its length.

Note that the terms frequency or cps are used above instead of the word pitch. Pitch is what the ear hears, but as was mentioned before, it is a relative term because the ear cannot actually count the number of vibrations per second.

The Second Law

This second law does not concern the length of the string, so that factor will now be constant. The only change made this time is on the amount of tension, or pull, on the string. This is, incidentally, what the piano tuner does when he turns the tuning pins. As the tension on the strings is increased, the frequency also increases.

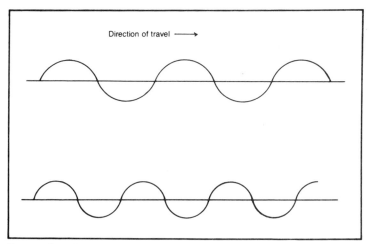

Fig. 2-5. Sound waves slightly out of phase.

It might be assumed that doubling the tension on a string should also double the number of cps with which it vibrates. In fact, the tension on the string must be increased to four times over what it was originally in order for the frequency to double. If the frequency is to be tripled, the tension must be nine times as great. This relationship is expressed mathematically by saying that the frequency is proportional to the square root of the tension.

The Third Law

This last law has to do with the effect on frequency of the string's mass per unit of length. The term mass should not be confused with weight. Mass is a measure of an object's density. Weight is a measure of its mass that has been multiplied by the force of gravity. Because gravity decreases with distance from the center of the earth, an object would have less and less weight as it was taken progressively farther from the earth's surface. Its mass would not change, however, because its size and density would remain the same. The terms mass and weight could be used interchangeably for practical purposes, if the object were left on the surface of the earth, but it is best to keep the two concepts separate.

The mass per unit of length of a piano wire is changed by varying the diameter of the wire. Because its density remains the same, increasing the diameter increases its mass. Experiments show that the frequency of a vibrating string is inversely proportional to the square root of its mass per unit of length. All other factors remaining constant, increasing the diameter of a string, and, therefore, its mass, will cause a decrease in the number of cps with which it vibrates.

Chapter 3

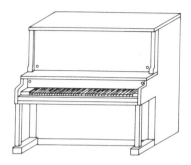

Sound and Music

As seen from the study of sound, each musical tone must be the result of a certain number of vibrations per second of the piano wire. Each key of the piano must then correspond to a string or group of strings that produce these vibrations when struck. Because the speed of the vibrations can be counted and expressed numerically in terms of frequency, the various tones in the musical *scale* must bear some mathematical relationship to each other. The Greek mathematician Pythagoras investigated these relationships. Because the Greeks agreed that certain tones sounded good together and some did not, he set about to discover what the relationships were that existed between the pitches which tended to sound pleasant when played together. He did this by studying the vibrations of a *monochord*, a single string stretched tightly above a resonating box.

Although he had no physical means for counting the number of vibrations, Pythagoras was able to discern the relationships of the pleasant tones by comparing the lengths of the strings involved. He expressed the relationships of the string lengths in terms of proportions or fractions. He found that the pitches that sound best when played together had the simplest proportional relationships. In other words, they could be expressed as simple fractions such as ½, ⅔, and ¾. The pitches that sounded less agreeable had more complex proportional relationships such as 8/9 or 8/15. These studies lead to an understanding of why the Greeks had enjoyed using certain pitches simultaneously and why they had chosen to limit their music to tones of eight basic pitches. This led to the development of the musical scale used presently in Western culture.

Other cultures developed musical frameworks different from that of the Greeks. Oriental music, for example, is based on a series of five basic tones. Because the music played in the West since the time of the Greeks was based on their eight tone system, discussion of the mathematical relationships of modern music will be concerned only with the eight tone scale.

SCALE DEFINED

The musical scale is more appropriately called a *tone ladder*. It is a series of musical tones, each bearing some mathematical relationship to the others. The modern scale is divided into 12 separate tones. Seven of these are given the letter names A through G and are found by playing the white keys of the piano (Fig. 3-1). The white keys are also called *naturals*.

The black keys are called either *sharps* or *flats* in music, but in piano tuning they are always referred to as sharps. A sharp gets its name from the natural key to its immediate left. Thus, considering the key G in Fig. 3-1, the black key to its right is called G sharp. The symbol # is used for the word sharp, so this note can be written G#. To the musician, this key could also be called A flat, depending upon

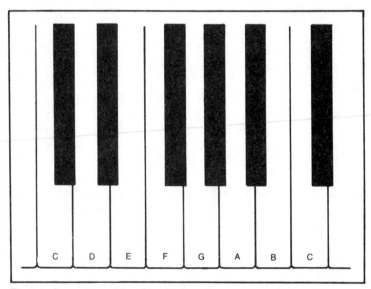

Fig. 3-1. One octave of the piano keyboard.

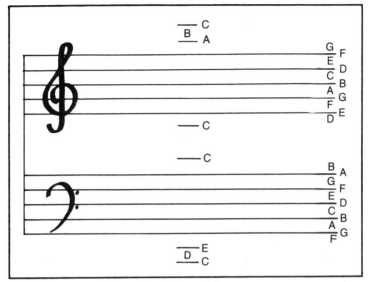

Fig. 3-2. Grand staff with treble and bass clefs.

how a piece of music is written. Modern tuning methods cause the G# to have the same frequency as A flat, which is why the black keys can all be referred to as sharps when discussing piano tuning.

The pattern of keys shown in Fig. 3-1 is repeated throughout the keyboard, so more than one key has the same letter name. In fact, at least seven keys have the same name. In order to identify any given key, some way of distinguishing between them is necessary. One way is to count how far a key is from the bottom of the keyboard. The lowest key becomes A1, the next, A#2 and so on. Because each key plays a different tone with a specific frequency, a key can also be identified by noting its proper frequency after its letter name. For example, the forty-ninth key from the bottom, which is an A, should have a frequency of 440 cps. This key can, therefore, be referred to as A440.

MUSICAL NOTATION

Once it is understood what the scale is and how it looks on the keyboard, a way is needed to represent it all on paper. Figure 3-2 shows the musical staff used for this purpose. The symbol on the left side of the upper part of the staff signifies that this is the treble clef, which assigns each line and space a letter name that represents a note of the scale. The symbol on the left of the lower part of the staff means this is the bass clef, which assigns a different letter name to

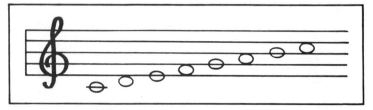

Fig. 3-3. Musical notation for playing a major scale beginning on C.

each line and space. As might be surmised, the treble clef contains tones that are higher than those represented on the bass clef.

The letter names, shown to the right in **Fig. 3-2**, are not normally found in written music. They are shown here only to identify the names of the lines and spaces. The short lines located above the bass clef and below the treble clef represent middle C. This is C40 on the piano keyboard.

The notes that are written on the staff show which tones of the scale, hence which notes of the piano keyboard, are to be played. Placing the symbol # next to a note indicates that the sharp of that note is to be played. Because the note on a written page represents both a key on the piano and a tone of the scale, the term note may be used to mean either a musical tone or the key of the piano that produces that specific tone.

Musical notation is read from left to right, so **Fig. 3-3** shows the playing of a major scale beginning at middle C. When notes on the staff are placed directly above and below each other, they are to be played at the same time. Figure 3-4 shows the notation for playing a group of notes simultaneously. A group of notes played together is called a *chord.* Chords are given specific names, which depend upon the notes that are played.

INTERVALS

An *interval* is defined as the frequency distance between any

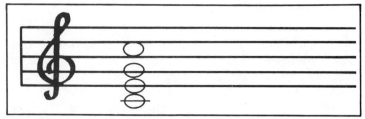

Fig. 3-4. Musical notation for playing a C Major chord.

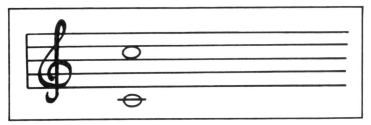

Fig. 3-5. The interval of an Octave.

two notes of the scale. As Pythagoras found, this frequency distance can be expressed as a ratio or fraction. The simplest interval in music is the Unison. This interval is the result of two tones, from separate sources, that are at the same frequency. An example is the three strings found in the piano for each note in the tenor and treble sections. The strings are tuned so that each will produce the same frequency when struck by the hammer. Because of this, they are called unison strings. The mathematical relationship between tones of a Unison is expressed as the ratio 1:1.

The next simplest interval, and the one on which the modern scale is designed, is the Octave. The tones of the Octave have the frequency ratio of 1:2, which is also expressed as the fraction ½. The Octave derives its name from the eight steps in the scale between the lowest note in the interval and the highest. Figure 3-5 shows an Octave from C40 to C52 represented in musical notation.

The interval shown in Fig. 3-6 is the next simplest. This interval, having the ratio 2:3, is called a Fifth because it encompasses five steps in the scale. The Fifth shown in Fig. 3-6 contains the notes C40 and G47. If a scale is played beginning at C40, G47 is the fifth note encountered.

The interval of the Fifth can be used to find all the notes of the scale that Western man has used in his music, namely the *diatonic scale*. Begin at any C on the piano and play a Fifth downward. Then

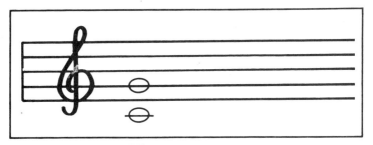

Fig. 3-6. The interval of a Fifth.

29

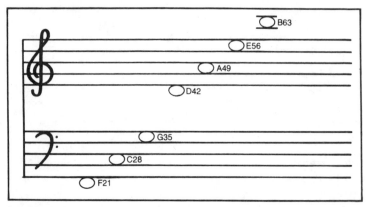

Fig. 3-7. The cycle of Fifths from which the notes of the scale can be derived.

start again at C and play a series of notes up the scale, each a Fifth higher than the one preceding. These tones, which spread over five octaves, comprise the notes of the diatonic scale as begun on C. They are shown in Fig. 3-7. Playing within this scale is called playing in the key of C.

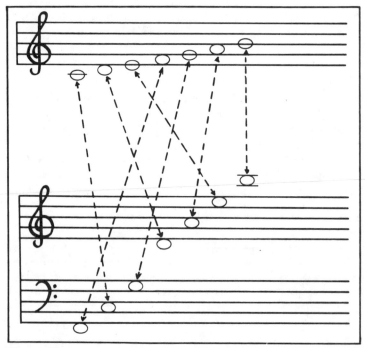

Fig. 3-8. The cycle of Fifths compressed into one octave

Table 3-1. Frequency Ratios of the Intervals of the Diatonic Major Scale.

Interval Name	Note	Frequency Ratio from C
First (Unison)	C1	1/1
Second	D	9/8
Third	E	5/4
Fourth	F	4/3
Fifth	G	3/2
Sixth	A	5/3
Seventh	B	15/8
Eighth (Octave)	C2	2/1

If these notes are compressed into the same octave, as shown in Fig. 3-8, they produce the scale used today. Pythagoras discovered the mathematical relationships between these tones, and they are shown in Table 3-1. These ratios apply to the frequency distance of the intervals. The ratios will be the same, no matter what note is used as the starting point.

The ratios given in Table 3-1 can be used to find the correct frequency for any note, providing the frequency of the first tone in the scale is known. For example, if C1 in Table 3-1 is known to be 266 cps, the frequency of F can be found by multiplying 266 by 4/3. the frequency of F would then be found to be 354.67 cps. The ratio of the frequencies of any two adjacent notes in the scale can be found by dividing their ratios relative to the first note in the scale into each other. As an example, suppose you want to find the ratio of the frequencies of E and F in Table 3-1. This ratio is found by dividing 5/4 by 4/3 which equals 15/16. This is the ratio of the frequencies of E and F. Table 3-2 shows the ratios that result when this is done for the entire octave.

Table 3-2. Ratios between Adjacent Tones in the Diatonic Major Scale.

Notes	Ratio Between Steps
C-D	8/9
D-E	9/10
E-F	15/16
F-G	8/9
G-A	9/10
A-B	8/9
B-C	15/16

Table 3-2 shows that there are three different ratios between the adjacent tones of the scale. Two of these are fairly close together, namely 8:9 and 9:10. At two places in the scale, the frequency difference is 15:16, which is smaller. If the scale is played, and the difference between each tone listened to carefully, it can be perceived that the sound interval between the second and third note and between the seventh and eighth note is less than elsewhere in the scale. This is what should be expected considering the smaller proportional difference that is found to exist mathematically at these places.

Because the ratios 8:9 and 9:10 are very close, the diatonic scale can be considered to be made of steps that have two basic frequency distances. Most of the steps, having the wider distance of either 8:9 or 9:10, are called whole steps or *whole-tones*. The smaller intervals are called half steps or *semi-tones*. The diatonic scale has eight steps, with a semi-tone difference between the third and fourth notes as well as between the seventh and eighth notes. The rest of the steps are a whole-tone apart. A look at the piano keyboard shows that its design accommodates this scale exactly when it begins on C. There are no sharp keys between the E and F or the B and C, where the semi-tone steps should fall.

What happens, though, if the scale is played beginning on D, this is to say, played in the key of D? If C1 in Table 3-1 is assigned the frequency of 264 cps, which is close to that of middle C, the frequencies of the other notes can be found by multiplying 264 by the appropriate ratios, which are given in the table. These are shown in Table 3-3. The frequency of D is found to be 297 cps.

Suppose now this figure is used, and the scale begun again, but this time starting on D. The second note in the scale is now E. Using the same ratios given in Table 3-1, its frequency is found to be 334 cps, which is different, but close to the frequency assigned it when played in the key of C. Therefore, if the piano had been tuned using

Note	Frequency
C1	264 cps
D	297 cps
E	330 cps
F	352 cps
G	396 cps
A	440 cps
B	495 cps
C2	528 cps

Table 3-3. Frequencies of the Tones in the Diatonic Major Scale Derived from the Ratios in Table 3-1, with C1 Assigned a Frequency of 264 cps.

C as the starting point, the E which serves as the Third from C could also serve fairly well as the Second from D.

Now, using D as the starting point at 297 cps, and multiplying this by 5/4, the frequency of the Third from D can be found to be 371 cps. The piano, which was tuned with C as the starting point, has no note tuned to this frequency. It falls between the F and G. To accommodate for this, the piano has a black key between the F and G, called here the F sharp. The other sharps, which are found on the keyboard and in the musical scale, are there so that a scale may be played on an instrument when starting with any note. No matter what the starting point, a scale can be played while maintaining the diatonic relationship of whole-tone and semi-tone steps by using a combination of white keys (naturals) and black keys (sharps).

The early Greeks did not have this flexibility. Because they had not fully developed the scale, they used a system called *modes*. Each mode had eight steps, and the placement of the whole-tone and semi-tone steps was specified as well as the pitch on which the mode was to begin. This must have presented some difficulty when changing from one mode to another because all the instruments would have to be retuned.

The pattern of Fifths, which was used to find the eight notes of the scale beginning on C, can be extended to find the sharps that are needed to play the diatonic scale in other keys. Figure 3-7 shows the cycle of Fifths developed no higher than B. Continuing from there, it is found that the Fifth above B is F#. A Fifth above that is C# and so on for the remaining G#, D#, and A#. The Fifth above A# turns out to be E#. There is, however, no E# key on the piano. Because a sharp is a semi-tone above a natural, and F is a semi-tone above E, F is played for E#. Because F was the starting point of the pattern, the cycle is completed.

So far, the scale that has been considered is the *diatonic major scale*. This is the do, re, mi scale that all children are familiar with. There are also *diatonic minor scales*. The minor scales are similar to the major scale, but the semi-tone steps fall in different places. Playing music in the minor scales results in a sound that is more moody or haunting. The uses and derivations of the minor scales are not really important to the piano tuner. He should, however, be able to find the minor Third interval because it is used in tuning. The minor Third falls a semi-tone below the Major Third.

It is important to realize that the two notes of a given interval are always spaced the same distance apart on the keyboard, regardless of where in the scale they are located. The piano tuner can

Table 3-4. The Number of Semi-Tones Within Each Interval Used in Piano Tuning.

Interval	Number of Semi-Tones
Octave	13
Major Sixth	10
Fifth	8
Fourth	6
Major Third	5
Minor Third	4

always find the second note of an interval by counting the correct number of semi-tones from his starting point. The intervals most commonly used by piano tuners are the Octave, Major Sixth, Fifth, Fourth, Major Third, and minor Third. Table 3-4 shows the number of semi-tones found within each of these intervals.

To use this table, it is necessary to count both the key on which the series begins and the one on which it ends, as well as all the sharps and naturals in between. As an example, suppose the Fifth above F# is to be found. The table shows that there are eight semi-tones in the interval of a Fifth. By beginning to count on F#, you find the eighth semi-tone above it to be C#. C# is then the Fifth above F#.

THE HARMONIC SERIES

Because sound is defined as the vibration of an object, much can be learned about why a piano string (actually a piece of wire) sounds as it does by studying the nature of its vibrations. If a string is stretched tightly between two fixed points and is plucked or otherwise induced to vibrate, it will begin to swing back and forth along its entire length, as shown in Fig. 3-9. This is the first mode of vibration, and it produces a tone called the *fundamental*, which is recognized as a note in the musical scale.

At the same time, the string will divide and vibrate in halves as

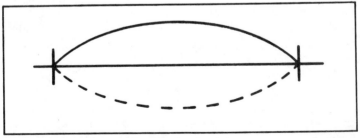

Fig. 3-9. The first mode of vibration of a piano wire.

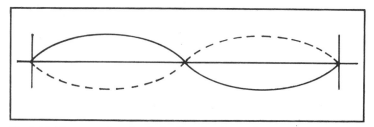

Fig. 3-10. The second mode of vibration of a piano wire.

shown in Fig. 3-10. Since the string is now vibrating in halves also, a second tone will be produced from this same string. The tone produced by this second mode of vibration will have twice the frequency of the sound produced by the first mode of vibration because the length of each segment is half that of the entire string. For example, if the string in Fig. 3-9 produces a tone with 440 cps, the tone produced by the second mode of vibration will be 880 cps. This tone is called the *second harmonic* of the string; it is much quieter than the fundamental. It is so quiet that it is not normally heard by the casual listener.

In addition to dividing and vibrating in halves, the string will also vibrate in three equal segments as shown in Fig. 3-11. This will happen at the same time that the two other modes are occurring. The string divides and vibrates in increasingly shorter sections, with each mode producing a separate distinct tone. All these tones occur simultaneously.

The *harmonic series* is the term used to describe this group of tones. The fundamental, caused by the string vibrating along its entire length, is called the *first harmonic*. The next highest tone, caused by the string vibrating in halves, has already been identified as the second harmonic. The next highest, caused by the string vibrating in thirds, is called the *third harmonic*. The *fourth harmonic* is caused by the string dividing in four equal segments, and so on. Suppose for example that the string in Fig. 3-9 is vibrating and producing a fundamental tone with a frequency of 65.406 cps, which is the frequency of C16. The second harmonic is always twice the

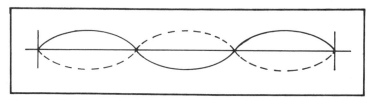

Fig. 3-11. The third mode of vibration of a piano wire.

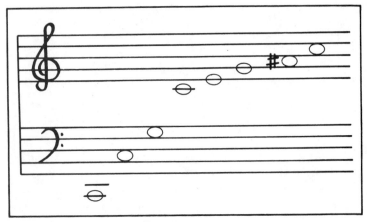

Fig. 3-12. The harmonic series of C16.

frequency of the fundamental, so in this example it would have a frequency of 130.812 cps, which is the same frequency as the fundamental of key C28.

Figure 3-12 shows the harmonic series that results from C16, as shown in musical notation. Each of these tones will correspond to the fundamental of some note on the keyboard. By playing these notes on the keyboard, the interval distances between the successive harmonics can be seen easily. They are shown in Table 3-5. These same interval distances will apply to the harmonic series of every note of the scale.

The harmonic series of two tones will have some frequencies that will coincide. Consider the harmonic series of C16 and G24. They are shown in Fig. 3-13. The second harmonic of G24 should have the same frequency as the third harmonic of C16. By listening

**Table 3-5. The Interval Distance
between Successive Frequencies in the Harmonic Series.**

Harmonic	Coincides with Note	Interval Distance from Preceding Harmonic
Eighth	C52	Second
Seventh	A#50	minor Third
Sixth	G47	minor Third
Fifth	E44	Major Third
Fourth	C40	Fourth
Third	G35	Fifth
Second	C28	Octave
First	C16	—

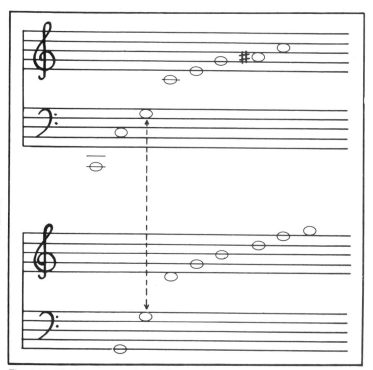

Fig. 3-13. The harmonic series of C16 and G24 showing the coincidental harmonics.

for the frequencies that should coincide in the harmonic series of two notes, a piano tuner can accurately tune a piano. To do this, he must listen for the beating that occurs when the notes are tuned so that the sound waves of their coincidental harmonics are slightly out of phase.

Consider again what happens when C16 and G24 are played at the same time. The harmonic series of each should overlap at certain frequencies. If C16 and G24 are tuned to their mathematically correct frequencies, then what is called a *pure* or *just* interval results. If these two notes are tuned to a pure Fifth, then the second harmonic of G24 will be 392.436 cps, and the third harmonic of C16 will also be 392.436 cps. The sound that results when both are played simultaneously will be smooth; almost as if made by one string. If, however, the G is tuned so that its second harmonic is 2 cps low, the sound the two produce together will not be smooth. Instead it will produce the alternating loud-soft pulsations of beats. Because the coincidental harmonics are 2 cps out of phase, the sound will beat two times in each second.

Consider now the interval of a Unison. The note A49, in the middle of the piano, has three strings. If two of the strings are plucked, each should vibrate with a fundamental of 440 cps. If one string is slightly low, producing for example a fundamental of 437 cps, the sound the strings produce together will beat three times in each second. If one string is too high by 3 cps, the resulting sound will still beat three times per second.

Although beating can be used to determine if a string is out of tune, it cannot be used to tell automatically if it is sharp or flat (i.e., too high in frequency or too low). It is enough to realize that the piano tuner does not have to play each string separately and then guess if it is at the same pitch as another. Two strings can be tuned, comparing one to the other, until the beats finally disappear. This is how pianos are tuned, so learning how to hear and count beats is absolutely essential. Suggestions on how to do this will be given later.

EQUAL TEMPERAMENT

The term *temper* means to modify or regulate. When tuning the piano, it is necessary to temper the diatonic scale because of some difficulties arising from the relationships of tones in it. The problem can be illustrated by tuning the piano beginning at A1 in two different ways.

First, A1 is tuned to its proper frequency of 27.5 cps. The rest of the A's are then tuned by Octaves from this starting point. Because the ratio of the Octave is known to be 2:1, the correct frequencies for the other A's can be figured quite easily. A1 is tuned to 27.5 cps, so this is multiplied by two to show that the frequency of A13 is 55 cps. This is then multiplied by two in order to find the frequency of A25, and so on. Upon reaching A85, which is the seventh in the series to be tuned, the correct frequency is found to be 3520 cps.

Beginning again at A1 having 27.5 cps, but this time using the ratio of successively higher Fifths, the tuning will once again arrive at A85. This time, calculations based on the ratio of 3:2 for Fifths indicate that A85 should have a frequency of 3568.024 cps. This means that the frequency of A85 would be about 48 cps higher if the tuning were done by Fifths instead of by Octaves. This discrepancy is known as the *comma* of Pythagoras. The term comma is defined as a small differentiation in pitch.

The nature of how this discrepancy affects the scale within one octave can be shown by comparing a scale designed with the frequencies figured from C and one figured from D. Earlier, when investigating the nature of scales, it was shown that sharps were needed in order to be able to play in any key. It was discovered that if C40 were arbitrarily set at 264 cps, then E44, which is a Third above C40, would have a frequency of 330 cps. If the scale is now started on D, the Second above it should be E44, a whole-tone. Calculations done using the ratio of 9/8 for the interval of a Second, show that E44 should now have a frequency of 334.1 cps. If these calculations are continued for the remaining intervals, the frequencies for the octave from D42 to D54 can be found. Table 3-6 shows the frequencies for the notes of this octave as figured from C40 at 246 cps, and as figured from D42 at 297 cps. In the second case, D42 is assigned the frequency of 297 cps because this is found by multiplying the frequency of C40 by 9/8. This is the mathematical ratio that should exist between these two when calculating the scale from C40.

Even though both sets of figures are determined by the perfectly legitimate means of multiplying by the intervals' ratios, the answers can be seen to vary, depending upon what note is used as a base for the calculations. It is evident then that no diatonic scale can be tuned on the piano by using only pure intervals. Because the piano locks the player into using combinations of 12 separate tones in each octave, the tuning must be altered from pure intervals, so that the instrument can be played in any key. This characteristic of the keyboard causes a *temperament* to be required. Instruments in the violin family, for example, have no such limitations. The violinist can make minute changes in tuning as he plays by changing slightly the position of his fingers. A singer can do the same by adjusting the tension of his vocal chords.

**Table 3-6. The Frequencies Derived from the
Diatonic Ratios for the Octave D42-D54 as Calculated from C40 and D42.**

Scale Beginning on D42 As Calculated from C40 at 264 cps		Scale Beginning on D42 As Calculated from D42 at 297 cps	
Note	Frequency	Note	Frequency
D54	594 cps	D54	594 cps
C#53	557 cps	C#53	556.9 cps
B51	495 cps	B51	495 cps
A49	440 cps	A49	445.5 cps
G47	396 cps	G47	396 cps
F#46	371.3 cps	F#46	371.3 cps
E44	330 cps	E44	334.1 cps
D42	297 cps	D42	297 cps

When tuning keyboard instruments, it is necessary to make some kind of compromise in the spacing of the intervals. Although this will result in some distortion, the result is an acceptable intonation with which any possible interval or group of intervals can be played and still sound pleasant to the ear. The inaccuracies that result from the necessary compromises are small, and, through time, Western culture has become accustomed to hearing this altered scale. It has become so accepted that it is considered by the modern listener to be accurate, and a scale built on pure intervals would sound odd to him. Even the violinist, who could alter his fingering to play pure intervals tends to use the tempered ones because they are what he is used to hearing.

The various systems that have been used through time to modify the diatonic scale have been called temperaments. An adjective is used to describe what type of temperament it is. Modern music is played in *equal temperament*, which was popularized by J. S. Bach. His studies on the well-tempered "clavier" are written to demonstrate the flexibility of this type of tuning.

To understand how an equally tempered scale is designed, consider again the ratios between the steps of the diatonic major scale as shown in Table 3-2. The ratio between whole-tone varies slightly, depending upon the location in the scale. Because a whole-tone is comprised of two semi-tones, the ratios of these will also vary throughout the scale. Equal temperament is used to eliminate this variation and to make the proportional distances between all semi-tones equal.

The end result is a scale in which the Fifths are all tuned a little bit narrow of a pure Fifth, but not so much as to be objectionable. The Fourths all end up being slightly wide of pure. All the intervals are affected; some tuned wide and others, narrow. None are so radically altered as to be dissonant, at least to modern man. The only exceptions are the Unisons and the Octaves. Unisons, being two tones of the same frequency, will always be pure no matter how the scale is tempered. Because the Octave is the basis for Western music and because the tempering that must be done takes place within this framework, the Octave remains pure.

To understand the theory behind equal temperament, remember that the frequency of the highest tone in the Octave is twice that of the lowest. Remember also that the frequency of one note is multiplied by the proper ratio to find the frequency for the other notes. Because the Octave contains 12 semi-tones and because equal temperament requires that the ratios between all 12 be equal,

Table 3-7. The Frequencies of an Equally Tempered Octave Compared with Those Derived from the Diatonic Ratios. Both Are Calculated from A49 at 440 cps.

Frequencies in Equally Tempered Scale from C40-C52. Based on Standard Pitch of A49 at 440 cps.		Frequencies of Diatonic Scale using Ratios Given in Table 3-3. Based on Standard Pitch of A49 at 440 cps.	
Note	Frequency	Note	Frequency
C52	523.251 cps	C52	528 cps
B51	493.883 cps	B51	495 cps
A49	440.000 cps	A49	440 cps
G47	391.995 cps	G47	396 cps
F45	349.228 cps	F45	352 cps
E44	329.628 cps	E44	330 cps
D42	293.665 cps	D42	297 cps
C40	261.626 cps	C40	264 cps

the proper ratio between adjacent semi-tones will be that number that equals two when multiplied by itself 12 times. This number is the ratio that can be expressed as the decimal 1.0594631.

Using the ratio 1.0594631 and the accepted convention that A49 should have a frequency if 440 cps, it is possible to assign frequencies to all the notes of the piano. Table 3-7 shows the frequencies that result from using this ratio for the Octave C40-C52. Also shown in Table 3-7 are the frequencies for these same notes when figured from the ratios of the diatonic scale, assuming that A49 is at 440 cps. Table 3-7 shows that the frequencies of the equally tempered scale are different from those derived solely from the diatonic ratios.

Piano tuners have established logical and relatively easy systems for tuning one Octave of the scale so that it is equally tempered. This Octave is then used as the starting point for tuning all the remaining notes of the piano. Two of these systems will be described in Chapter 6.

Chapter 4

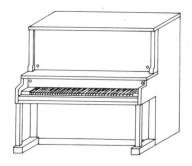

Piano Tuning Tools

The tools that are used to work on the piano can be divided into three groups. These tools are used for tuning, regulating, or repairing. Tools used for tuning and regulating are specialized and must be purchased from a company that supplies piano technicians. Many of the tools used for repairing are available in hardware stores. It is not necessary to purchase a large number of expensive tools, so those that are used should be of the best quality. The extra expense of top quality tools will pay for itself in saved time. Using tools of poor quality can make a job very difficult, if not impossible.

TUNING TOOLS

The following tools, which are shown in Fig. 4-1, will be needed when tuning the piano: tuning hammer, tuning fork, felt temperament strips, and rubber mutes. The most important of these tools is the tuning hammer. This is a misleading name because it is not really a hammer and should never be used as such. It is really a wrench. The handle is 10-12″ long, with a head and tip at one end that is designed to fit onto the tuning pins. It is imperative to use the best quality hammer and tip, even when learning to tune the piano. The so-called student tuning hammer is sometimes so poorly made that even an experienced tuner has trouble achieving good results. The best hammers have a head that screws onto the handle. Tips of various sizes can then be secured to the head.

Although a one-piece head and tip unit can be bought, the

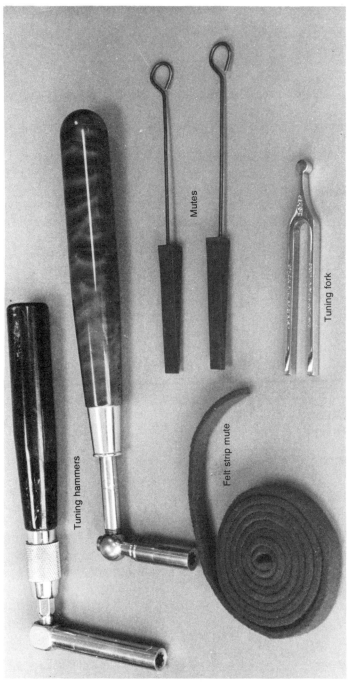

Fig. 4-1. Tuning tools (photograph by Rich Strader).

43

ability to change tips is preferable. It is sometimes necessary to change tips in order to accommodate fatter, or thinner, tuning pins. It may also be necessary from time to time to use a longer tip so that the handle will clear a part of the piano's case. It is a good idea to use the shortest head and tip combination possible, so a long tip would only be used when case dimensions dictate. When purchasing a head for the tuning hammer, it is best to have the handle as close to 90 degrees to the head as possible, although heads with different angles can be bought.

The gooseneck style hammer should definitely be avoided. Instead of having a separate head and tip, this hammer is all one piece, with the handle bending at one end to form the head and tip. This type of tuning hammer is too flexible at the bend to allow good control of the tuning pin. The head and tip, being at right angles to the handle, need to form a strong, inflexible unit with it. This will give the tuner the greatest control over the tuning pin.

The extension tuning hammer needs to be considered. This style has a rod that fits inside the handle and that can be pulled out several inches to make the handle longer overall. This feature may be helpful when tuning the old square grands, which require the tuner to have a long reach because the tuning pins are located at the back of the instrument. For general use though, the handle need never be extended. A 10" handle will provide sufficient leverage for good tunings. Extension hammers tend to be heavier than nonextension models, and this extra weight may be of some advantage when using certain types of tuning techniques. It must be remembered that the hammer will be lifted off and on tuning pins several hundred times during the course of one tuning. The extra weight may be annoying if it causes the hand and arm to tire from moving the hammer from pin to pin.

The importance of using the highest quality tip cannot be too heavily stressed. Tips of poor quality may not fit securely on the pin, allowing the hammer to wobble excessively. A firm fit is desirable in order for the piano tuner to effect the fine movements of the tuning pin that are necessary for accurate tuning. Poor quality tips may even have burrs that will scratch the tuning pins, making a secure fit even more difficult on subsequent tunings.

The next most important tool of the tuner is the tuning fork. From the beginning, the student should strive to tune all pianos to standard pitch, which is to have A49 at a frequency of 440 cps. The temptation to tune the piano at whatever pitch it is found should be resisted. Even though this may save some time and energy, this practice would result in pianos getting progressively lower in pitch. This overall lowering of pitch is harmful to the piano, and in the end it will be harmful to the tuner and his business. The use of a tuning fork is essential for keeping pianos at the proper pitch.

The most expensive type of tuning fork is not really a fork at all. It is an electronic device that produces a tone of the proper pitch. These devices can be set to produce any tone in the chromatic scale over a range of several octaves. The main advantage of this type of tool is that it produces an easily heard, sustained tone that does not die away after a few seconds as the tone from a tuning fork does. These pitch generators are very accurate, but one pays dearly for the accuracy and the ability to produce any tone in the scale.

This latter feature is not necessary. It may even tempt the student into trying to set the temperament octave by matching tones with the generator. This practice would result in a poor temperament and, therefore, a poor tuning overall. It is simply impossible to accurately match the tones and produce a good temperament. Even if the tones could be matched accurately, a good temperament would not be assured. Pianos are unique, and the frequencies that produced a good temperament in one instrument may need to be adjusted to produce an equally good temperament in another. While this type of tool may have applications helpful to the experienced tuner in certain situations, it will be detrimental to the student if he never learns to tune a good temperament because he has relied upon the pitch generator and the false sense of security it provides.

The next most sophisticated type of tuning fork is actually a bar placed over a resonant box. The bar is struck with a mallet, in the manner of a xylophone. The tone produced is louder and sustains longer than the tone of a tuning fork, but the advantage gained may not be worth the higher cost. In most cases, one can learn to use a tuning fork in such a manner as to get a very accurate tuning, which is after all the point of using the fork in the first place.

A good tuning fork is all that is needed to ensure a good tuning at the proper pitch. The best forks can be counted on to be very accurate, providing they are properly cared for. The tuning fork should be kept in a case to protect it from nicks and dents, which could affect its accuracy. Rust, dirt, and deposits from fingers can also affect the pitch of the fork, so it should be kept clean. The metal the fork is made of will contract and raise the pitch if it is left in cold weather for any length of time. For best results, the fork should always be at room temperature when used.

Piano tuners work by tuning just one string at a time. Since most notes have three strings, it is necessary to have some method for stopping the sound normally produced by the strings with which the tuner is not working. For example, if he is tuning the middle string of a treble note, the tuner will have to silence the two outside strings.

Several tools are used for this purpose. The most common are rubber mutes and strips of felt called *temperament strips.* The latter can be used to mute entire groups of strings simultaneously. Rubber mutes, on the other hand, must be moved constantly to deaden different strings as the tuner moves about through the scale of the piano. Mutes may be bought with wire handles, which are convenient as they allow easier placement of the mute. The type of muting system used is a matter of individual choice. Each person should experiment with various methods to determine which seems the most comfortable.

During the initial practice exercises presented in this book, the student will be instructed to use rubber mutes to deaden just a few strings at a time. Later, when the total tuning process is considered, a method for muting the entire piano with temperament strips will be presented. When doing a complete tuning, muting the entire piano is a time-saving, effective method. During initial practice, though, it can be confusing and is unnecessary. This is the reason for starting with rubber mutes and switching later to the temperament strips.

Mutes and temperament strips are very inexpensive, and the student should buy several different types so that he may experiment to find which suits him best. When placing the initial order with a tuners' supply company, it is also advisable to buy at least one strip of felt called action felt. This can be purchased in strips 52" long and 1" wide. Action cloth of medium thickness is an excellent material for muting the treble section of the piano. Instructions for using it as a treble muting strip will be given later.

REGULATING TOOLS

These tools are specially designed to adjust the different parts of the piano action. Figure 4-2 shows the basic tools used when working on both vertical and grand actions. Some of these are used to adjust special screws; others bend wires which action parts are attached to. The use of each tool will be discussed in the chapters on regulation.

Most of these tools are designed to fit into a common handle. It

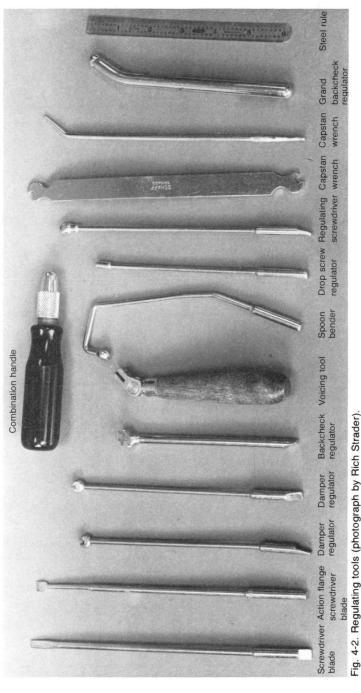

Fig. 4-2. Regulating tools (photograph by Rich Strader).

Screwdriver blade · Action flange screwdriver blade · Damper regulator · Damper regulator · Backcheck regulator · Voicing tool · Spoon bender · Drop screw regulator · Regulating screwdriver · Capstan wrench · Capstan wrench · Grand backcheck regulator · Steel rule

Combination handle

47

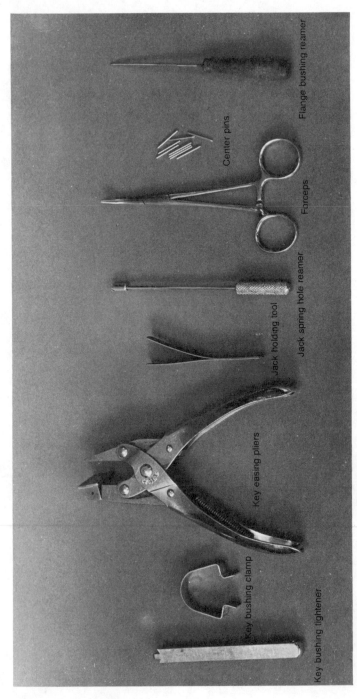

Fig. 4-3. Repair tools (photograph by Rich Strader).

Flange bushing reamer

Center pins

Forceps

Jack spring hole reamer

Jack holding tool

Key easing pliers

Key bushing clamp

Key bushing tightener

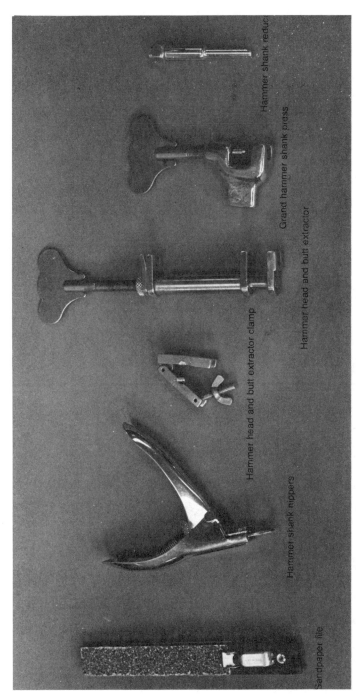

Hammer shank reducer

Grand hammer shank press

Hammer head and butt extractor

Hammer head and butt extractor clamp

Hammer shank nippers

Sandpaper file

Fig. 4-4. Repair tools (photograph by Rich Strader).

49

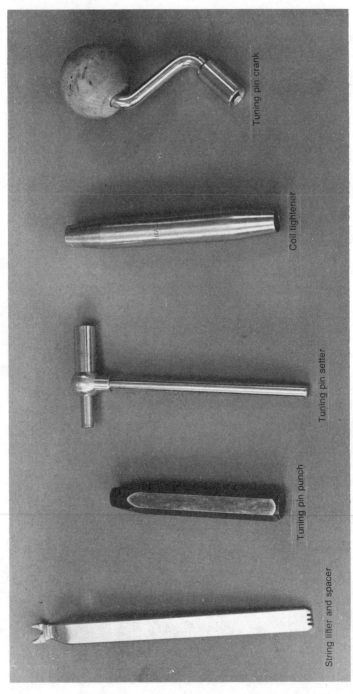

String lifter and spacer

Tuning pin punch

Tuning pin setter

Coil tightener

Tuning pin crank

Fig. 4-5. Restringing tools (photograph by Rich Strader).

is a good idea to have more than one of these handles so that several tools can be used at the same time. The screwdriver blades that fit into these handles have one advantage over the types of screwdrivers normally available in hardware stores. These blades are made with round shanks of small diameter. When repairing and regulating a piano action, it is often necessary to work with the screwdriver blade inserted between closely spaced action parts. The shanks of most good screwdrivers not made especially for piano technicians are square and are designed for strength. The squared shanks can catch on action parts and damage them. Because strength is not so important when working on a delicate piano action, the small round shanks work much better.

REPAIRING TOOLS

A world of fine, expensive tools made especially for repairing pianos can be purchased, but a few good, simple ones will normally do just as well. Basic repairing tools, which can be found in hardware stores, might include the following: a needle-nose pliers, 5-inch vise grips, Phillips head screwdriver (for removing case parts), small ball peen hammer, music wire cutters with compound leverage, a micrometer, and a variable speed drill.

The most commonly used repairing tools that must be bought from a piano technicians' supply company are shown in Fig. 4-3 and Fig. 4-4. Tools that are used when replacing strings in the piano are shown in Fig. 4-5. Again, proper use of these tools will be explained, when necessary, in Chapter 9.

PIANO TECHNICIANS' TOOL CATALOGS

In order to buy many of these tools, it will be necessary to obtain a catalog from a company that supplies parts and tools to piano technicians. Because these companies sell only to those in the tuning profession, send a business card when requesting a catalog. If a business card is not available, most will supply a catalog to anyone who writes and explains he is studying piano tuning.

Get as many of these catalogs as possible and leaf through them, studying the various tools and supplies that are available. Studying these catalogs is a good way to learn the names of the tools and parts that are used in tuning and repairing the piano. It also gives you a feeling for the scope and complexity of the trade that can be reached by those who choose to pursue it as a profession. Many of the tools available are quite specialized and are not needed by the average piano tuner. A list of companies that supply piano technicians is in the Appendix.

Chapter 5

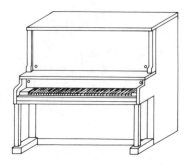

Tuning Exercises

The first exercises in tuning will involve tuning two of the three strings that form the unison group. In order to do these exercises, one of the strings will need to be muted, leaving the other two free to vibrate. A rubber mute is used for this and is placed in such a manner as to silence the right-hand string of each group of three. This is done by inserting it between two groups of unison strings (Fig. 5-1). The mute must be placed high enough along the string so that it does not impede the motion of the hammer. Except for this consideration, it is not important where along the length of the string the mute is placed. It should always be inserted firmly between the two groups of strings in order to effectively damp the sound of the string. It can be seen that the mute will silence two strings; one from each group of unisons.

When working on the following exercises, practice will take place on the group to the left of the mute. By always working in this manner, it will be easier to keep the tuning hammer on the correct pin. Once the use of the mute is understood, several other factors need to be considered. They are the position of the person at the piano, the position of the tuning hammer on the tuning pin, the position of the hand on the tuning hammer, how to move the hammer in order to achieve the best results, and how to set the tuning pin in order to have a stable tuning.

POSITION OF THE TUNER AT THE PIANO

The student first needs to decide whether to sit on the bench or

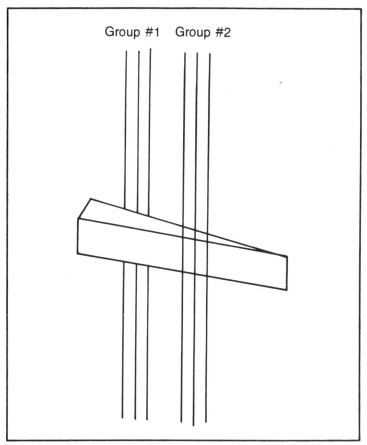

Fig. 5-1. Muting the right-hand string of unison group #1.

stand while tuning. This decision will depend somewhat on the sizes of the piano and the person. Most tuners prefer to sit when working on the smaller vertical pianos. Tall uprights and grands may require the tuner to stand. Again, this decision depends upon the physical limitations of the individual.

Whether the tuner sits or stands, he should be in a comfortable position and be well braced by leaning against the piano or otherwise keeping his body as immobile as possible. When standing, the feet should be about shoulder width apart. The tuner can lean against the key slip. When sitting, both feet should be placed firmly on the floor. Keeping his body from moving unduly will allow the tuner to make the delicate arm movements necessary for accurate tuning.

POSITION OF THE TUNING HAMMER ON THE TUNING PIN

The tuning hammer should be placed on the pin so that the handle is above the head and tip and is as close to vertical as possible. Keeping the handle oriented vertically minimizes the possibility of bending a tuning pin by leaning on the handle of the hammer. If the tuner is tuning with his right hand, he can incline the

Fig. 5-2. Correct right-hand position for raising pitch in a vertical piano (photograph by Rich Strader).

Fig. 5-3. Correct right-hand position for lowering pitch in a vertical piano (photograph by Rich Strader).

handle slightly to the right, and vice versa if he is using his left hand.

POSITION OF THE HAND ON THE TUNING HAMMER

In general, the hand should be placed near the end of the handle in a position that will allow the tuner to have the best control over the hammer. The right-handed tuner can raise the pitch of a vertical piano by placing his hand as shown in Fig. 5-2. When lowering the pitch, it will be necessary to turn the right hand over as shown in Fig. 5-3. Figure 5-4 shows an alternate hand position that can be used when lowering the pitch with the right hand. With the hammer cradled in the crook of the hand, and the fingers on top of the pin block, a slight squeeze of the hand will raise the handle and lower the pitch. This position is very useful when making the final minute movements used to tune a string.

Fig. 5-4. Alternate right-hand position for lowering pitch in a vertical piano (photograph by Rich Strader).

Fig. 5-5. Correct left-hand position for raising or lowering pitch in a vertical piano (photograph by Rich Strader).

If the left hand is used, it should be placed on the hammer as shown in Fig. 5-5. This position can be used for either raising or lowering pitch. When raising pitch, the heel of the hand pushes against the handle. Lowering the pitch requires only that the hand be opened slightly and that the fingers be squeezed gently toward the palm of the hand. It is advantageous to be able to tune with either hand, so the student should try with both hands, regardless of which is his predominate way of tuning.

Tuning a grand piano requires a different hand position because the pinblock is oriented horizontally. Figures 5-6 and 5-7 show how the hammer should be held when tuning a grand. The hand can be left in the positions shown whether raising or lowering the pitch of a string. The leverage is applied with either the fingers or the heel of the hand.

MOVEMENT OF THE TUNING HAMMER

The tuning hammer should always be moved so that the handle of the hammer follows an arc that is parallel to the plane of the pinblock. This type of motion will turn the pin and not put any pressure on it that would bend it. Besides the possibility of bending the pin, force that is applied in such a manner as to push the pin from side to side will cause compression of the wood in the pinblock. This will result eventually in loose and jumpy tuning pins. The extent of the motion of the tuning hammer should be only that needed to turn the pin.

The actual turning of the pin can be done in one of two ways. It can be turned slowly and steadily, back and forth, until it stabilizes with the string at the proper pitch. The alternative is to turn the pin with small sharp movements of the tuning hammer. The idea of these small movements is to move the pin through a turn of only a few degrees with each motion of the hammer. This method seems to be the best one to use when working on a piano with a tight pinblock. When using the slow, steady method on a tight pinblock, the high moment of inertia that must be overcome before the pin will turn causes it to turn too far when it finally does move. Whichever method is used, it is wise to move the pin through a very small arc with each movement of the hammer, because there is a tendency to turn it too far.

SETTING THE TUNING PIN

Setting the pin refers to certain techniques the tuner must use to stabilize the tuning of a string. Even when a string has been tuned to the proper pitch, it may not stay there if this step is not done. Setting the pin is done by first raising the pitch of the string two or three beats per second above the desired frequency and then lowering it while striking the key sharply. This practice of always tuning from above will help insure stability of the tuning.

Setting the pin is necessary because of the mechanical nature

Fig. 5-6. Correct right-hand position for raising or lowering pitch in a grand piano (photograph by Rich Strader).

59

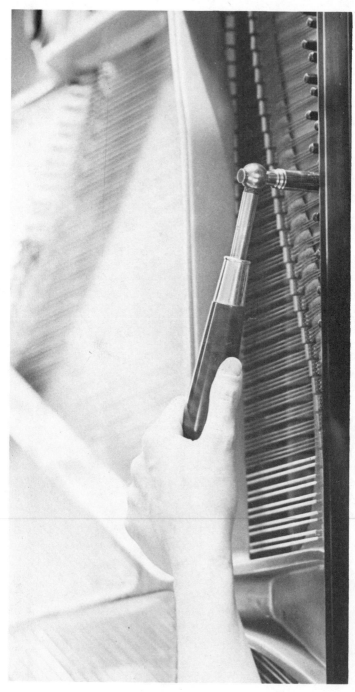

Fig. 5-7. Correct left-hand position for raising or lowering pitch in a grand piano (photograph by Rich Strader).

of the string and the pinblock. When a string is raised in pitch, the force needed to turn the tuning pin may put a slight twist in the part of the pin inside the block. If the string is simply pulled up to pitch, the twist will work out when the piano is played, causing the string to drop in pitch. Tuning slightly sharp and lowering it will remove any twist that may have occurred.

Setting the pin in the manner described is also necessary in order to equalize the tension on the string over the bridges. To understand what this means, what happens when the tuner begins to raise the pitch of a string must be realized. Initially, the string will begin to stretch between the pin and the upper bridge. Because of friction at the bridge, the string will not actually begin to slide across the bridge until some stretching of the short upper portion of the string has occurred. Next, the string will begin to move across the upper bridge, and under the capo, and will also begin to stretch along its speaking length. The speaking length of the string is that part that actually produces the sound (i.e., the part between the two bridges.) The tension on the top part of the string will continue to be greater than that of the speaking length. The last part of the string to stretch will be that from the lower bridge to the hitch pin. If the tuner simply raises the pitch of a string and proceeds to the next note, he will leave unequal tensions along its length, as shown in Fig. 5-8. As the piano is played, the tensions will equalize over the bridges, causing the string to go out of tune.

Normally, setting the pin requires that the string be raised only a few beats per second sharp before lowering it to the correct pitch. It may be necessary to raise a string even higher at first if its tuning pin is not very tight in the pinblock. The key should be struck sharply just as the string is being lowered. The sharp blows on the key will cause the string to vibrate strongly. This will effectively lower the friction at the bridge and allow the string tensions to equalize more readily. The key should be struck at least as hard as it will be when the piano is played, but pounding on the piano unmercifully is not necessary.

TUNING EXERCISES: UNISONS

With the above information in mind, the actual practice of tuning can begin. The first exercises should consist of tuning two unison strings to the same pitch. First, the right-hand string of the unisons must be muted. The left-hand string should then be pulled flat. This should be done slowly, listening for the pulsating sound of the beats, which should get faster as the string is pulled flatter. It

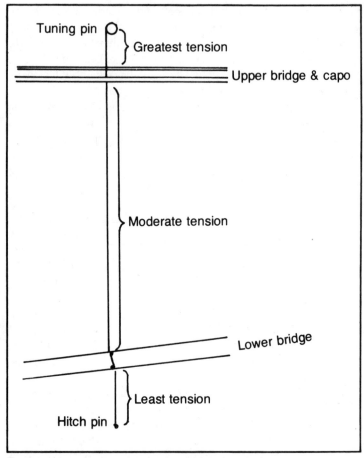

Fig. 5-8. Unequal string tensions after raising pitch.

may be difficult to hear the beats at first. The sound may be easier to hear with one ear than the other or if the head is moved around to different positions. Closing the eyes to avoid distractions may also be helpful.

After the string has been lowered a little, it should be brought up on pitch, again slowly. As the string being tuned gets closer to the frequency of the middle string, the beats will become slower and slower, disappearing altogether when the two strings are at the same frequency. As the left hand string is raised above the pitch of the other, the beats will once again appear, getting progressively faster as the string is raised higher in pitch. Again bring the string lower until the beats slow and finally disappear, meaning that the unison is pure or, in other words, that the two strings have the same frequency.

This exercise should be repeated several times in order to get accustomed to the sound of the beats as they slow down when approaching a pure unison and then speed up again as unison is passed. No attempt should be made at this time to actually tune the strings. It is more important to simply become familiar with the sound of the beating. When doing this exercise, try nodding the head or making some other physical motion that matches the speed of the beating.

It is important to change frequently to different notes in order to avoid fatiguing the ear. It is best to change to a note that is not close to the one used previously. For example, practice on a C for a few minutes. Then switch to an F. Then change to a D and from there to a G. It is best to confine this practice to the octave above the wound strings because the beats are most easily heard in this part of the piano.

The ear will tire quickly at first, and it may be impossible to work for more than a few minutes. When this happens, the ears should be rested for a while. Walk away from the piano and then return to it a few minutes later. Many short breaks will be needed at first, and the length of time one is able to work before needing a rest may be distressingly short. Length of working time will increase with time and practice. Working at first for too long a period of time only increases frustration and does not help the learning process. When hearing the beats becomes too difficult, take the needed break and return to the piano with a rested ear. Many short practice periods will accomplish more than one long session that leaves the student fatigued and frustrated.

Close attention to the work being done can reduce two major frustrations of beginning tuners. Remembering to move the mute when changing from note to note is necessary. Trying to hear beats when all three strings are free to vibrate will only cause problems because the third string may well be out of tune with the others and will beat against them. Care in placing the tuning hammer will eliminate the problem of turning the wrong tuning pin. Finding the correct pin may seem confusing at first, and time should be spent to make sure the hammer is on the right one. Besides wasting time and energy, turning the wrong pin can result in broken strings.

This initial exercise also provides the time to learn the feel of the tuning hammer. Practice turning the tuning pin the smallest amount possible. Lower the pitch of the left-hand string until it is about the same as the note that is a semi-tone lower in the scale. Try to make many small movements when bringing the pitch back up to that of the unison string. Try to make as many as 15-20 separate movements of the pin when raising the pitch one semi-tone. This type of practice will help eliminate the tendency to turn the pin too far.

Eventually, begin practicing actual tuning of the left-hand string. Remember first to bring it sharp in relation to the middle string and then to lower its pitch until the beats disappear. Strive from the beginning to set the pin so that the tuning will be stable. To see if the tuning is stable, lean the hammer lightly to the left and then push it lightly to the right. If the pin is properly set, and the tuning stable, no beating will begin when the hammer is pushed lightly in either direction. If there is any doubt, strike the key sharply five or six times. If the string does not go out of tune, then the pin has been correctly set.

These exercises should be practiced diligently. Learning to tune a pure Unison is important since it is the basic interval. Tuning the other intervals to pure will be much easier once the student has mastered tuning good, pure Unisons. The exercises will do two things if they are done religiously. First, they will develop hand coordination. Second, they will teach the ear how a pure interval should sound. The most difficult part of developing hand coordination will be learning not to turn the pin too far. With practice, the hand will be able to feel the tuning pin as it begins to turn and the string as it slips over the bridges. Strength and endurance will also be developed.

Ear training can be difficult at first. Ideally, the harmonics of two unison strings should be identical. This is not always the case because one or more of the higher harmonics may be at slightly different frequencies. This will cause some beating in the higher harmonics even though the lower ones may be pure. The student must learn to ignore the higher harmonics and concentrate on listening to the lowest tone in the harmonic series. Remember that the lower harmonics are the loudest and should be most easily heard.

TUNING EXERCISES: OCTAVES

After some facility has been accomplished in tuning Unisons, attention should be turned to practice in tuning other intervals. Initially this should be restricted to tuning Octaves. Practice on the Unisons should not stop, but should be continued with the intervals.

64

Alternating octave and unison tuning practice may help cut down on ear fatigue.

In order to tune an Octave, two strings of each note will need to be muted. This can be done by using four mutes. Figure 5-9 shows how the mutes can be inserted between unison groups so that only the middle string of the note being tuned is left free to vibrate. It is easier though to begin using a temperament strip at this time because it will then be possible to concentrate on tuning practice instead of on moving mutes. The temperament strip is inserted between groups of unisons as shown in Fig. 5-10. This will leave only the middle string of each group free to vibrate. The strip mute can be inserted with a screwdriver or the handle of a wire handled mute. The narrow end of the strip is placed at the right end of the tenor section where there is less room between the capo and the hammer's strike point. It is not important where along the length of the string the strip is inserted, so long as it does not interfere with the hammers. At this time it is only necessary to mute the tenor section of the piano because practice will be limited to this area.

Begin the practice of tuning Octaves by tuning C52 to C40. For the purposes of the exercise, it does not matter if C40 is at the correct frequency. To tune the Octave, the two notes must be played simultaneously. Put the hammer on the correct pin of C52 and play it and C40 at the same time. Listen for the beating as was done with the Unisons. Concentrate on hearing the beating that is occurring at the pitch of C52. This beating is caused by the second harmonic of C40 and the fundamental of C52, which should be at the same frequency when the Octave is pure. Try to ignore the higher coincidental harmonics that will also be beating, but more quietly.

Begin by slowly lowering the pitch of C52. If the speed of the beating increases, then the interval was too narrow initially, meaning that C52 is lower in pitch than it should be. Slowly raise the pitch of C52 and listen as the beats slow down and then speed up again as the pure interval is passed. It is important to keep playing the two notes over and over in order to be able to hear the beats because they will die away quickly. After the pitch of C52 has been raised so that it is sharp of a pure Octave, but only a few beats per second sharp, gently lower the pitch. The beats will slow, then disappear, meaning the interval is pure. Remember to always set the tuning pin.

The beats of an interval being tuned will become very difficult to hear once pure is approached. This is because the beating will become very slow. It is very difficult to distinguish a pure interval

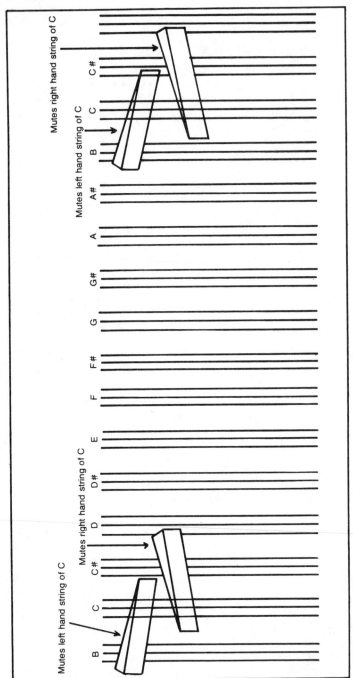

Fig. 5-9. Using four mutes to silence all but the middle strings of two notes being tuned.

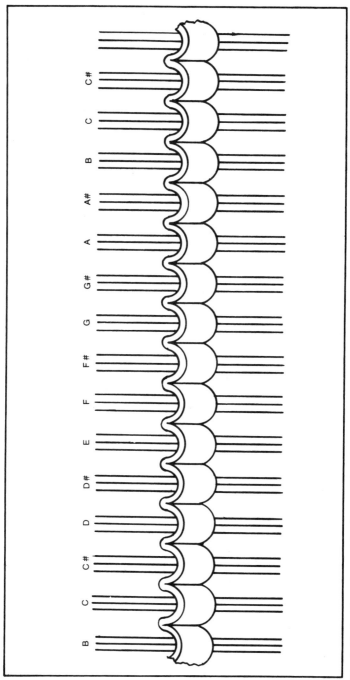

Fig. 5-10. A strip mute used to silence all but the middle strings of a series of unison groups.

from one that is beating once every two or three seconds. When tuning Octaves, a piano tuner can use several tests to determine if the Octave is indeed pure. These tests will be discussed thoroughly in Chapter 7. Two will be presented here, though, so that practice in using them may begin.

Both tests involve comparing the speed of the beating of two different intervals. These intervals will include the two notes of the interval being tuned and another note called the *test note*. Again consider the Octave C40-C52. Once C52 has been tuned, the tuner can check the accuracy of his work by using a minor Third-Major Sixth test. To do this, D#43 is used as the test note. D#43 is used because it is a minor Third above the lower note of the Octave. The interval from D#43 to C52 is a Major Sixth. When the Octave is indeed pure, the minor Third will beat at the same speed as the Major Sixth.

The octave tuning can be double-checked by using a Major Third-Major Tenth test. For this, G#36 is the test note. It is chosen because it is a Major Third below C40 and a Major Tenth below C52. When the Octave is pure, these two intervals will beat at the same speed. Practice using these two tests should begin as soon as the first attempts at octave tuning are made. The tests work even if the test notes are not at their correct frequencies relative to the notes of the Octave.

Two requirements must be met before the test will work. For the minor Third-Major Tenth test, the minor Third must be slightly narrow of a pure interval. With the Major Third-Major Tenth test, the Major Third must be slightly wide of a pure interval. In either case, if there is a doubt, roughly tune the test note until the beats disappear when it is played simultaneously with the lower note of the Octave. Then pull it flat until beating can be heard easily. This is usually when the interval is beating around five or six times per second.

When practicing the tuning of Octaves, use the same jumping around type of pattern as was used when practicing Unisons. First tune a C to C Octave, then an F to F, back to a D to D, and so on. As with Unisons, this will help cut down on ear fatigue. Tune the Octaves for a few minutes; then return to tuning Unisons. After a short time on the Unisons, return to Octaves once more.

TUNING EXERCISES: FOURTHS AND FIFTHS

Eventually practice should include the tuning of Fourths and Fifths. The initial attempts should consist of attempting to tune these intervals so that they are pure. After some facility has been acquired with this, try first tuning them pure and then narrowing them until they beat about once each second. Learning to hear and count these slow beats will be necessary before attempting to tune a temperament. A visual aid can be helpful when learning to count these slow beats. A digital watch is an excellent aid because most have some sort of indicator that counts off each second. Watch the pulsating of this indicator and try to match the speed of the beating to it.

These exercises will teach the student how to hear and count beats and will help develop the coordination necessary to tune the piano. Practice should continue on these fundamentals even after the student has progressed to tuning temperaments.

Chapter 6

Tuning the Temperament Octave

Two systems have been devised for tuning the equally tempered octave that is used to begin a piano tuning. One system, which I prefer, involves tuning a cycle of Fifths and Major Thirds. The other system consists of tuning a cycle of Fifths and Fourths. The procedure for tuning a temperament octave by Fifths and Major Thirds will be presented first.

Whichever method is used, several assumptions apply to the tempered scale in general, regardless of how it is being tuned. The temperament octave is always located in the middle of the piano because this is where the beats are most easily heard and counted. The methods described in this chapter begin at C40 and encompass the octave F33-F45. It should be noted that some tuners, using an A440 tuning fork to begin the procedure, prefer to tune the octave from A37 to A49. The Major Thirds in the upper portion of this octave beat so rapidly that counting them is very difficult. This is why I chose the lower octave F33-F45.

Remember from Chapter 3 that all Fifths in the equally tempered scale must be tuned slightly narrow of pure and that all Fourths must be tuned slightly wide of pure. In the part of the scale being used for the temperament octave, each Fifth should be narrowed so that it will beat three times in five seconds. Each Fourth should be tuned wide so that it will beat five times in five seconds (or once each second) as was practiced in Chapter 5.

The first note of the temperament, C40, is tuned to the

C523.25 tuning fork. Tuning a string to a fork can be difficult because of the difference in the timbre of each. Using the fork properly will help minimize the problems encountered. The tuning fork should be struck firmly against the underside of the keyboard or against the knee. It may even be struck by a mallet made of a heavy hammer from the bass end of a grand piano. The fork should never be hit against anything metal because this may dent it and change its pitch. Once the fork is vibrating, its base should be placed against a large resonant surface, such as the *fallboard* or side of the piano. Placing the base of the fork against such a surface will make the sound loud enough to hear, since the large surface will amplify the quiet sound the fork emits.

As the base of the fork is placed against the resonant surface, the note to be tuned should be played. Count the beats and then try to tune the note to eliminate any beating. It will, unfortunately, be necessary to put the fork down while the tuning is being done. Pick it up again to check the tuning that was done. The sound of the fork dies away quickly, so it must be struck often when checking the accuracy of the tuning.

Both methods of tuning the temperament will be presented with the assumption that a temperament strip mute has been inserted throughout the tenor section of the piano and that only the middle string of each group of unisons has been left undamped. This means that only the middle string and the middle tuning pin of each group is being considered at this time. Later, the outside strings will be tuned to the middle string.

In order to tune the temperament, the tuner must count the beats of the coincidental harmonics of two different notes. He must know at what pitch the beating will be heard because there are several coincidental harmonics in the harmonic series of two notes. The tuner is concerned with the lowest of these. The frequency of the important coincidental harmonics will be the same as the fundamental of some note on the keyboard. This will be referred to as the *reference note* for the interval being tuned.

Take, for example, the notes C40 and G47. The third harmonic of C40 should be at the same frequency as the second harmonic of G47. This will be at the frequency of 783.8 cps, which is also the frequency of the fundamental of G59. Therefore, G59 becomes the reference note for the tuning of the Fifth C40-G47.

To use the reference note as an aid to tuning, play it several times and try to remember its pitch. Then stop playing it and play the two notes of the interval. Listen for the beating that will be at the same pitch as the reference note just played. This procedure may need to be repeated several times before the beating of the interval is heard well enough to be counted.

The term *tuned note* refers to the last one that was tuned. This will be used to tune the next note in the cycle. The tests that are described are simply ways to check the accuracy of a note being tuned.

TUNING THE TEMPERAMENT BY FIFTHS AND MAJOR THIRDS

This system of temperament tuning is designed so that all intervals will be tuned slightly sharp of pure. Because the Fifths are narrowed in equal temperament, when tuning Fifths, the note being tuned will be lower in the scale than the tuned note. Fourths and Major Thirds are wide in equal temperament, so when they are tuned in this system the note being tuned will be higher in the scale than the tuned note. The terms up and down will logically refer to which direction in the scale the next note to be tuned will be found. Down a Fifth from C40 is F33. Up a Fourth from C40 is F45, and so on.

Using this system of Fifths and Major Thirds to tune the temperament has two advantages. One advantage is that there are always tests for each note being tuned, once a groundwork of five notes has been tuned. There are no tests for the accuracy of these first five notes. The other advantage is that the fast beating of the Major Thirds is much easier to hear than the slower beating of the Fourths and Fifths. The Major Thirds in the octave being tuned (F33-F45) beat from 6 to 12 times per second. It takes some practice to recognize these fast beat speeds. Before trying to tune the temperament, the student should practice learning the speeds involved. This can be done by using a visual aid as was done before. Try tapping the finger the required number of times in each second. The beat speeds that must be learned are 5-6 times per second, 8-9 times per second, and 11-12 times per second. These are the speeds of the three Major Thirds that will be tuned as a groundwork. The speeds of the remaining Major Thirds can simply be compared to these. Once some familiarity with these speeds has been developed, the student can begin tuning the temperament using the sequence described below.

A key principle of equal temperament that makes this tuning system very effective concerns the Major Thirds. Their beat speeds get progressively faster as one plays successively higher Major Thirds in the scale. The Major Third F#34-A#38, for example, beats slightly faster than F33-A37 and slightly slower than G35-B39. This lets the tuner produce a very accurate temperament by making sure each Major Third beats faster than the next lower one and slower than the next higher one.

Each note to be tuned will be given with the note to which it is tuned and the reference note used to find the pitch of the beating. Any tests will also be given. The tuned note, note to be tuned, reference note and tests will also be shown in musical notation.

Step 1:   Tuning C40

  Tuned Note: Tuning Fork C523.25

  Note To Be Tuned: C40

  Beat Speed: 0 (pure)

  Test: Roughly tune G#36 so that it beats between three and seven times per second when played with C40. Compare the beat speed of G#36-C40 with that produced when G#36 is played while the tuning fork is sounding. The beat speeds should be identical when C40 is properly tuned.

Step 2:   Down a Fifth (Fig. 6-1)

  Tuned Note: C40

  Note To Be Tuned: F33

  Reference Note: C52

  Beat Speed: 3 times in 5 seconds—sharp

  Test: None

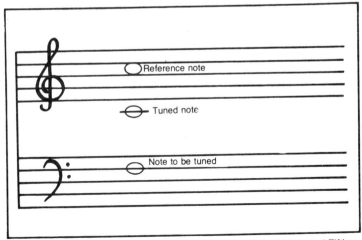

Fig. 6-1. Step 2 of tuning the temperament octave by Major Thirds and Fifths.

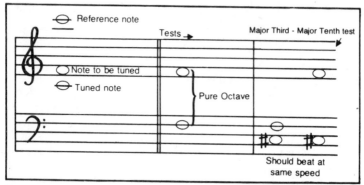

Fig. 6-2. Step 3 of tuning the temperament octave by Major Thirds and Fifths.

Step 3:   Up a Fourth (From C40 —Fig. 6-2)
    Tuned Note: C40
    Note To Be Tuned: F45
    Reference Note: C64
    Beat Speed: 5 times in 5 seconds—sharp
    Test: Octave F33-F45 should be pure. Check octave with
        Major Third-Major Tenth Test. C#29 is used as the
        test note.

Step 4:   Up a Major Third (From F33 —Fig. 6-3)
    Tuned Note: F33
    Note To Be Tuned: A37
    Reference Note: A61
    Beat Speed: 6 times per second—sharp
    Test: None

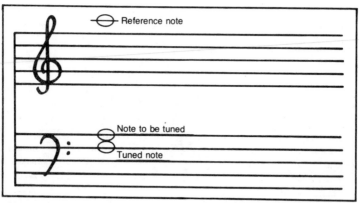

Fig. 6-3. Step 4 of tuning the temperament octave by Major Thirds and Fifths.

Step 5: Up a Major Third (Fig. 6-4)
    Tuned Note: A37
    Note To Be Tuned: C#41
    Reference Note: C#65
    Beat Speed: 8 times per second—sharp
    Test: Major Third C#41-F45 should beat 12 times per second

These five notes form the foundation from which the rest of the temperament octave is tuned. It should be noted that the beat speeds given for the three Major Thirds (F33-A37, A37-C#41, and C#41-F45) are the mathematical theoretically correct speeds. When working on a piano, especially the shorter ones, it may be necessary to deviate from the theoretical, usually by making the intervals beat slower. They must, however, keep the same sort of relative ratio of beat speeds. Each Major Third should beat about half again as fast as the next lower one. If there seems no way of approaching the correct speeds, recheck the accuracy of the octave F33-F45. It may not be pure, but slightly narrow instead. This is checked with the Major Third-Major Tenth test and the minor Third-Major Sixth test. It may even be necessary to tune the octave slightly wide, but not so much that noticeable beating can be heard.

Step 6: Down a Fifth (Fig. 6-5)
    Tuned Note: C#41

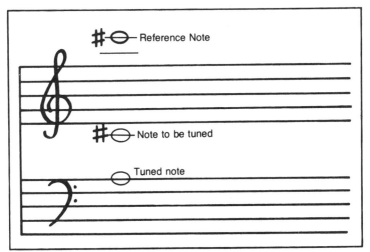

Fig. 6-4. Step 5 of tuning the temperament octave by Major Thirds and Fifths.

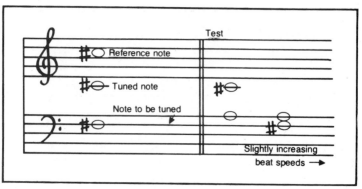

Fig. 6-5. Step 6 of tuning the temperament octave by Major Thirds and Fifths.

Note To Be Tuned: F#34
Reference Note: C#53
Beat Speed: 3 times in 5 seconds—sharp
Test: Compare the beat speeds of the minor Third F#34-A37 to the Major Third A37-C#41. The minor Third should beat slightly faster than the Major Third.

Step 7: Up a Major Third (Fig. 6-6)
    Tuned Note: F#34
    Note To Be Tuned: A#38
    Reference Note: A#62
    Beat Speed: Slightly faster than F33-A37
    Test: Fourth F33-A#38 should beat once each second. The Fourth should be slightly wide of a pure interval, meaning that A#38 should be slightly sharp of pure.

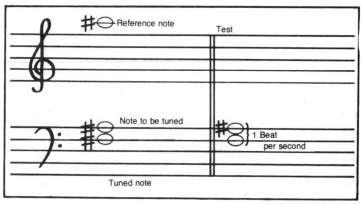

Fig. 6-6. Step 7 of tuning the temperament octave by Major Thirds and Fifths.

76

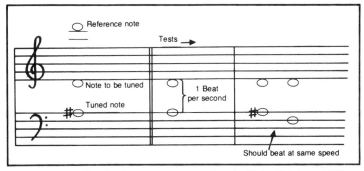

Fig. 6-7. Step 8 of tuning the temperament octave by Major Thirds and Fifths.

Step 8:   Up a Major Third (Fig. 6-7)
    Tuned Note: A#38
    Note To Be Tuned: D42
    Reference Note: D66
    Beat Speed: Slightly faster than A37-C#41
    Test: Fourth A37-D42 should beat once each second. Com-
        pare the beat speeds of the Major Third just tuned
        (A#38-D42) with the Major Sixth F33-D42. Both
        should beat at about the same speed.

Step 9:   Down a Fifth (Fig. 6-8)
    Tuned Note: D42
    Note To Be Tuned: G35
    Reference Note: D54
    Beat Speed: 3 times in 5 seconds—sharp
    Test: Fourth G35-C40 should beat once each second. Com-
        pare the beat speeds of the minor Third G35-A#38 and
        the Major Third A#38-D42. The minor Third should
        beat slightly faster than the Major Third.

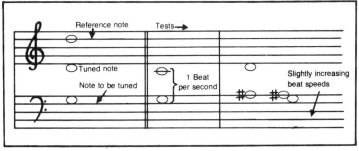

Fig. 6-8. Step 9 of tuning the temperament octave by Major Thirds and Fifths.

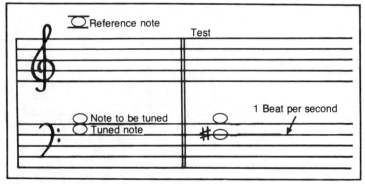

Fig. 6-9. Step 10 of tuning the temperament octave by Major Thirds and Fifths.

Step 10:   Up a Major Third (Fig. 6-9)
    Tuned Note: G35
    Note To Be Tuned: B39
    Reference Note: B63
    Beat Speed: Slightly faster than F#34-A#38 and slower than
                  A37-C#41
    Test: Fourth F#34-B39 should beat once each second.

Step 11:   Up a Major Third (Fig. 6-10)
    Tuned Note: B39
    Note To Be Tuned: D#43
    Reference Note: D#67
    Beat Speed: Slightly faster than A#38-D42 and slower than
                  C#41-F45
    Test: Fourth A#38-D#43 should beat once each second.
          Compare the beat speeds of the Major Third B39-
          D#43 and the Major Sixth F#34-D#43. They should
          beat at about the same speed.

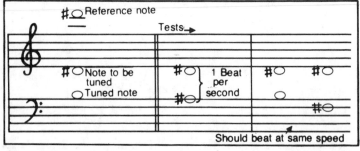

Fig. 6-10. Step 11 of tuning the temperament octave by Major Thirds and Fifths.

Step 12: Down a Fifth (Fig. 6-11)
    Tuned Note: D#43
    Note To Be Tuned: G#36
    Reference Note: D#55
    Beat Speed: 3 times in 5 seconds—sharp
    Test: Fourth G#36-C#41 should beat once each second. Compare the beat speeds of the minor Third G#36-B39 to the Major Third B39-D#43. The minor Third should beat slightly faster than the Major Third. Major Third G#36-C40 should beat slightly faster than the Major Third G35-B39 and slightly slower than A37-C#41.

Step 13:   Up a Major Third (From C40 —Fig. 6-12)
    Tuned Note: C40
    Note To Be Tuned: E44
    Reference Note: E68
    Beat Speed: Slightly faster than B39-D#43 and slightly slower than C#41-F45
    Test: Fourth B39-E44 should beat once each second. Fifth A37-E44 should beat 3 times in 5 seconds. Compare the beat speeds of the major Third C40-E44 and the Major Sixth G35-E44. They should both beat at about the same speed.

A properly tuned temperament octave should exhibit the following qualities that can be used to check the overall tuning. All Fifths within the octave should beat three times in five seconds. All Fourths should beat once each second. As the Major Thirds are played up the scale, they should slowly increase in beat speed, with each successively Major Third beating slightly faster than the one immediately below it. The same pattern of increasing beat speeds applies to ascending Major Sixths. Each successively higher diminished minor Seventh chord should beat slightly faster than the next lower one. A diminished minor Seventh chord is made up of four notes, each a minor Third apart. Figure 6-13 shows the diminished minor Seventh chords that are located in the temperament octave.

Because each piano is a unique instrument with individual characteristics, there may be minor differences in how the temperament octaves are tuned on different pianos. For example, the Fifths and Fourths may need to be tuned closer to pure than indi-

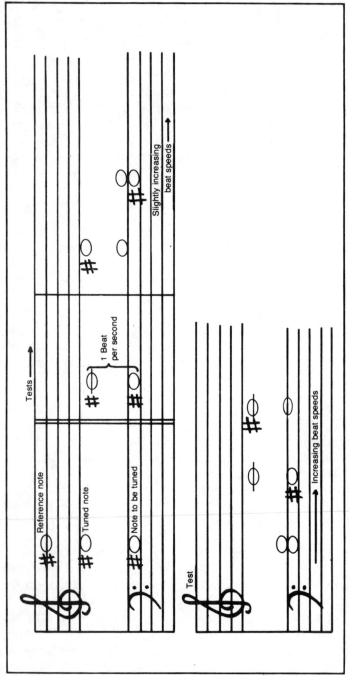

Fig. 6-11. Step 12 of tuning the temperament octave by Major Thirds and Fifths.

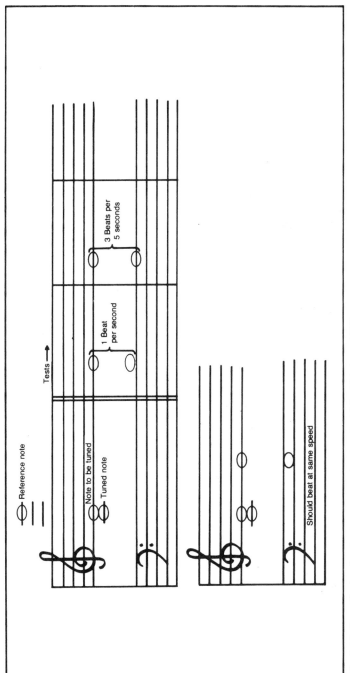

Fig. 6-12. Step 13 of tuning the temperament octave by Major Thirds and Fifths.

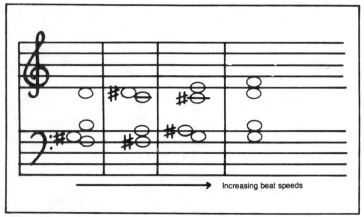

Fig. 6-13. The diminished minor Seventh chords that are found within the temperament octave.

cated and the beats speeds of the first three Major Thirds may need to be somewhat slower, especially on the smaller pianos. Regardless of the minor changes that must be made in the tuning of each piano to produce a good temperament octave, the above qualities should exist in every temperament tuned.

TUNING THE TEMPERAMENT OCTAVE BY FIFTHS AND FOURTHS

The alternate method of tuning a temperament octave involves tuning a series of Fifths, which are tuned up the scale, and Fourths, which are tuned down the scale. Because Fifths are narrowed in equal temperament and Fourths are widened, all notes tuned in this system will be tuned so they are slightly flat of pure. The only exception is the first interval, which is a Fifth tuned down the scale.

Step 1:   Tuning C40
          Tuned Note: Tuning Fork C523.25
          Note To Be Tuned: C40
          Beat Speed: 0 (pure)
          Test: Roughly tuned G#63 so that it beats between 3 and 7 times per second with C40. Compare the beat speed of G#36-C40 with that produced when G#36 is played while the tuning fork is sounding. The beat speeds should be identical.

Step 2:   Down a Fifth (Fig. 6-14)
          Tuned Note: C40

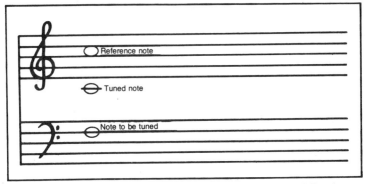

Fig. 6-14. Step 2 of tuning the temperament octave by Fifths and Fourths.

       Note To Be Tuned: F33
       Reference Note: C52
       Beat Speed: 3 times in 5 seconds—sharp
       Test: none

Step 3:   Down a fourth (from C40 —Fig. 6-15)
       Tuned Note: C40
       Note To Be Tuned: G35
       Reference Note: G59
       Beat Speed: Once each second—flat
       Test: None

Step 4:   Up a Fifth (Fig. 6-16)
       Tuned Note: G35
       Note To Be Tuned: D42
       Reference Note: D54

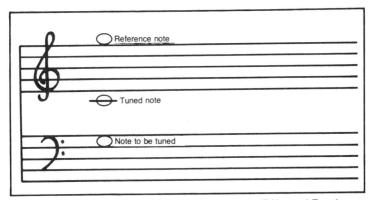

Fig. 6-15. Step 3 of tuning the temperament octave by Fifths and Fourths.

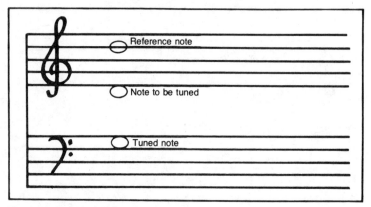

Fig. 6-16. Step 4 of tuning the temperament octave by Fifths and Fourths.

Beat Speed: 3 times in 5 seconds—flat
Test: None

Step 5:   Down a Fifth (Fig. 6-17)
      Tuned Note: D42
      Note To Be Tuned: A37
      Reference Note: A61
      Beat Speed: Once each second—flat
      Test: Major Third F33-A37 should beat about 6 times in each
            second.

Step 6:   Up a Fifth (Fig. 6-18)
      Tuned Note: A37

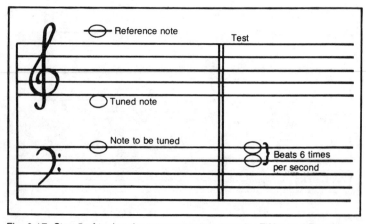

Fig. 6-17. Step 5 of tuning the temperament octave by Fifths and Fourths.

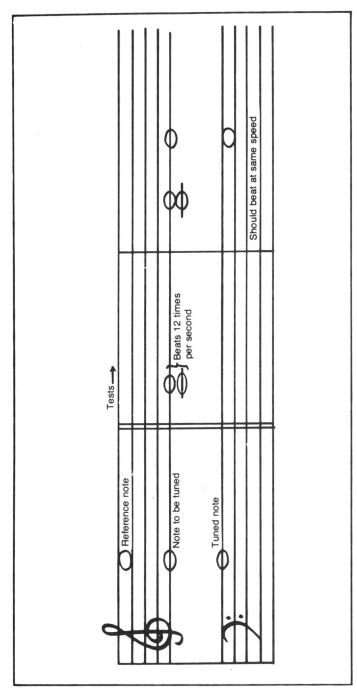

Fig. 6-18. Step 6 of tuning the temperament octave by Fifths and Fourths.

85

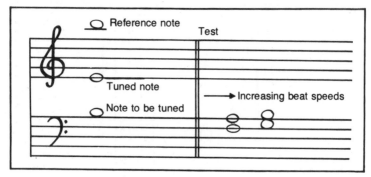

Fig. 6-19. Step 7 of tuning the temperament octave by Fifths and Fourths.

Note To Be Tuned: E44
Reference Note: E56
Beat Speed: 3 times in 5 seconds—flat
Test: Major Third C40-E44 should beat very rapidly, about 12 times in each second. Compare the beat speeds of the Major Third C40-E44 and the Major Sixth G35-E44. They should beat at about the same speed.

Step 7:   Down a Fourth (Fig. 6-19)
    Tuned Note: E44
    Note To Be Tuned: B39
    Reference Note: B63
    Beat Speed: Once each second—flat
    Test: Major Third G35-B39 should beat faster than the Major Third F33-A37. G35-B39 should beat about 7-8 times per second.

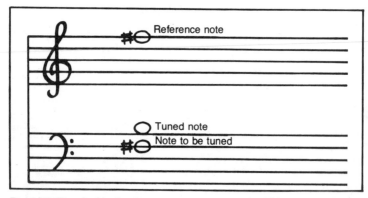

Fig. 6-20. Step 8 of tuning the temperament octave by Fifths and Fourths.

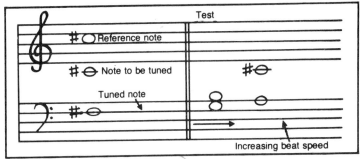

Fig. 6-21. Step 9 of tuning the temperament octave by Fifths and Fourths.

Step 8:   Down a Fourth (Fig. 6-20)
        Tuned Note: B39
        Note To Be Tuned: F#34
        Reference Note: F#58
        Beat Speed: Once each second—flat
        Test: None

Step 9:   Up a Fifth (Fig. 6-21)
        Tuned Note: F#34
        Note To Be Tuned: C#41
        Reference Note: C#53
        Beat Speed: 3 times in 5 seconds —flat
        Test: Major Third A37-C#41 should beat faster than G35-
                B39. A37-C#41 should beat about 8-9 times per sec-
                ond.

Step 10:   Down a Fourth (Fig. 6-22)
        Tuned Note: C#41

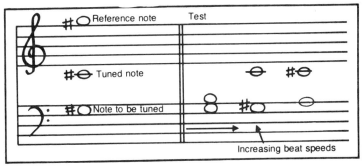

Fig. 6-22. Step 10 of tuning the temperament octave by Fifths and Fourths.

87

Note To Be Tuned: G#36
Reference Note: G#60
Beat Speed: Once each second—flat
Test: Major Third G#36-C40 should beat slightly faster than G35-B39 and slightly slower than A37-C#41.

Step 11:   Up a Fifth (Fig. 6-23)
Tuned Note: G#36
Note To Be Tuned: D#43
Reference Note: D#55
Beat Speed: 3 times in 5 seconds—flat
Test: Major Third B39-D#43 should beat slightly slower than C40-E44. Compare the beat speed of the Major Third B39-D#43 to the beat speed of the Major Sixth F#34-D#43. They should beat about the same speed.

Step 12:   Down a Fourth (Fig. 6-24)
Tuned Note: D#43
Note To Be Tuned: A#38
Reference Note: A#62
Beat Speed: Once each second—flat
Test: Major Third A#38-D42 should beat slightly faster than A37-C#41 and slightly slower than B39-D#43. Compare the beat speeds of the Major Third A#38-D42 and the Major Sixth F33-D42. They should beat at about the same speed. Fourth F33-A#38 should beat once each second.

Step 13:   Up a Fifth (Fig. 6-25)
Tuned Note: A#38
Note To Be Tuned: F45
Reference Note: F57
Beat Speed: 3 times in 5 seconds—flat
Test: Major Third C#41-F45 should beat slightly faster than C40-E44. The octave F33-F45 should be pure. Fourth C40-F45 should beat once each second. Compare the beat speeds of the Major Third C#41-F45 and the Major Sixth G#36-F45. They should beat at about the same speed.

With this system a different sequence of notes is tuned, but the same 13 notes are tuned, and the temperament octave should

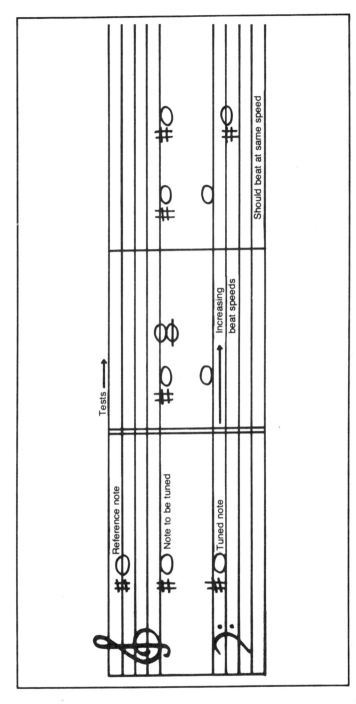

Fig. 6-23. Step 11 of tuning the temperament octave by Fifths and Fourths.

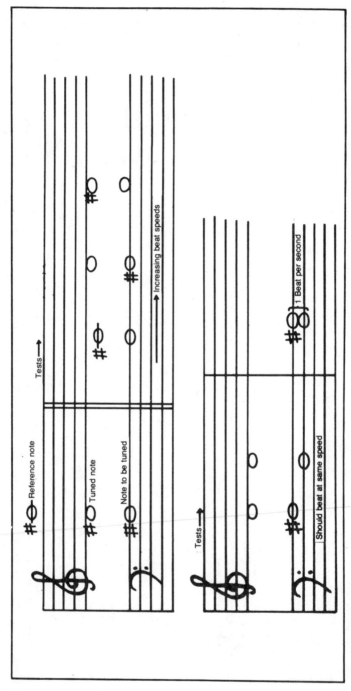

Fig. 6-24. Step 12 of tuning the temperament octave by Fifths and Fourths.

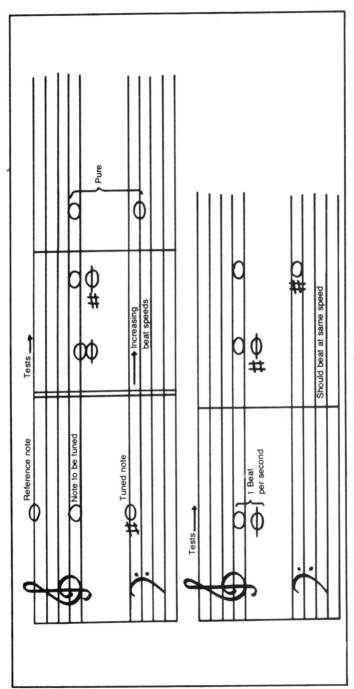

Fig. 6-25. Step 13 of tuning the temperament octave by Fifths and Fourths.

91

exhibit the same general characteristics that were described previously. Even though the system of Major Thirds and Fifths is preferred, both systems are presented. The student should eventually become familiar with both because a given piano may be easy to tune with one system and very difficult with the other. Initially, however, practice should be limited to the systems of Major Thirds and Fifths. Practice should not begin on the other system until the first one has been mastered. Practice should continue on unison and octave tuning while temperament tuning is being perfected.

Chapter 7

Tuning the Piano

The process of tuning the piano begins with the tuning of the temperament octave. Once this has been done, work can proceed to the rest of the piano. Using the temperament octave as a starting point, continue tuning by octaves. A number of tests are used to ensure this is done accurately. For example, once the temperament octave has been tuned, the next note tuned would be F#46, using F#34 as the tuned note. This is done by listening to the speed of the beats produced when playing F#34 and F#46 at the same time. Comparing the harmonic series of each note, it can be seen that the second harmonic of F#34 is at the same frequency as the fundamental (first harmonic) of F#46.

The beating of these coincidental harmonics should be listened to. Other coincidental harmonics of these two notes will be audible, but these will be higher in pitch and quieter and should be ignored. Only the fundamental of the higher note and the second of the lower one should be considered. Octaves are tuned pure, so there should be no beating of these harmonics when the octave is properly turned. Several tests can be used to be sure the octave is indeed pure. These will be discussed later in this chapter.

The rest of the notes up the scale of the piano are then tuned in the same manner as F#46. Because the middle section of the piano had been muted with the temperament strip when working on the temperament octave, tuning can proceed on the middle string of each note until reaching the treble stringing break. Then a decision must be made as to how to mute and tune the piano above the break. Two methods can be considered. One method uses rubber mutes and involves tuning all three strings of a unison before proceeding to the next note. The other involves using a strip mute, inserted in the same manner as the temperament strip, so that the middle string of each note can be tuned first. It is then necessary to return to each note to tune the unison strings.

TUNING WITH A MUTE

Beginning with the note above the stringing break, a rubber mute is inserted between the middle and right-hand strings (Fig. 7-1). The left-hand string is then tuned to the note one octave lower, which has already been tuned. Once the left-hand string is tuned, the mute is moved to the position shown in Fig. 7-2, the same position used when first practicing unison tuning. Now the middle string can be tuned to the left-hand string. Once these two are tuned so there is no beating, the mute is removed, and the right-hand string can be tuned to the other two. At first, it may be difficult to tune the right-hand string to two open strings. If this happens, the

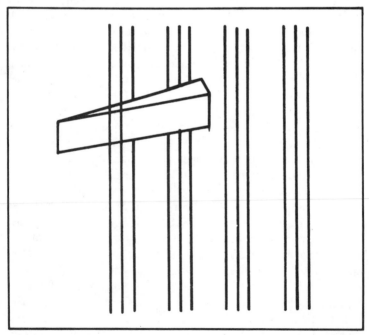

Fig. 7-1. Using a mute to silence the middle and right-hand strings of a unison group.

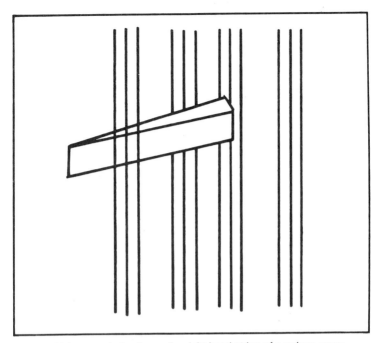

Fig. 7-2. Using a mute to silence the right-hand string of a unison group.

mute can be reinserted so that it silences the left-hand string, allowing the right-hand string to be tuned to the middle one alone.

Once all three strings have been tuned, the mute is then used in the same manner to tune the three strings of the next higher note in the scale. It is always a good idea, after all three strings have been tuned to check once again the tuning of this octave. This check is to make sure that the tuning has not slipped while working on the unison strings. Using this method, the tuner can proceed up the scale until all the strings of the treble have been tuned. Attention can then be turned to the bass.

The bass notes of the piano have two strings, except for the lowest notes, which have only one. The mute is inserted so that only the right-hand string of the note being tuned is left open (Fig. 7-3). This is tuned to the note that is one octave higher. The mute is then removed so that the left-hand string can be tuned to the other one. This procedure can be followed while tuning down the scale until reaching the single bass strings where no muting is needed.

The advantage of using mutes is that all the strings of each note can be tuned before proceeding to the next so there is no need to go back over the piano to tune unison strings. The disadvantage is the

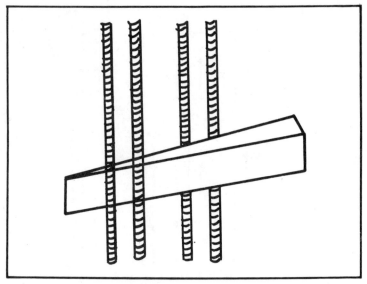

Fig. 7-3. Using a mute to silence one string of a bass unison group.

extra time used in moving mutes. That time might be better spent on tuning. The use of a strip mute eliminates the need to constantly move mutes.

TUNING WITH FELT STRIP MUTES

Besides the temperament strip, which is used in the middle section of the piano, another type of strip mute can be used when tuning the treble section. The problem with using a strip mute here is the small amount of space between the bridge and the uppermost dampers. Once the strip is in place, there is not sufficient room for the hammers to strike the strings. In order to make room, after having been inserted first above the dampers, the strip mute must be carefully slid between the dampers and the strings.

Begin at the highest note of the piano and work down the scale inserting the strip between groups of unisons. Upon reaching the highest dampers, the strip is placed between the tops of the dampers and the bridge. After the strip has been placed all the way to the stringing break, the dampers are pulled away from the strings, and the strip mute is slid down behind them. The grain of the damper felt runs parallel to the face of the damper, so care must be taken not to catch the felt on the muting strip as it is slid behind them because the damper felt might tear. Once the strip mute is in place, the right- and left-hand strings willl be muted. The middle one will be free to vibrate on every note.

Normally, the felt sold as temperament strips is too thick to fit between the dampers and the strings. A strip of action felt, 1″ wide and 52″ long can be used instead. Several thicknesses of this are available, but the medium thickness works best. It will effectively damp the treble strings and will fit easily behind the dampers. Because of the short length of the strings of the highest notes, it may be necessary to cut the action felt strip so that it is narrower than 1″ at one end. This end can be used at the extreme treble and will ensure enough room for the hammers to hit the strings.

With the strip in place, the middle string of each note is tuned up the scale until the top of the piano is reached. The top note presents a minor problem because the strip mute cannot be used to silence the right-hand string. A rubber mute can be used on this note. Inserting it between the middle and left-hand strings will leave the right-hand string free to vibrate. It is tuned first, and then the other two tuned to it. Once the highest note has been tuned, it will be necessary to remove the muting strip and reinsert it in a way that will allow one of the unison strings to be tuned to the middle string. When removing the strip care must be taken to avoid damaging the damper felts.

The strip mute is reinserted between every other group of unison string (Fig. 7-4). This is started by inserting the strip between the unison groups of note A#86 and B87. Because all three strings of C88 have already been tuned by using a rubber mute, the first string to be tuned is the right-hand string of B87. Tuning down the scale, left- and right-hand strings are tuned alternately.

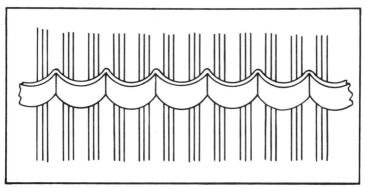

Fig. 7-4. Using a strip mute to silence one string in each of a series of unison groups.

This pattern might seem to cause some problem with getting the hammer on the correct tuning pin. If the pins are considered in groups of six, a pattern of pins to be tuned is seen, eliminating any confusion. The tuning pins in the treble are usually found in the configuration shown in Fig. 7-5. Each group of six tuning pins can be divided into three groups. The first group contains the two pins to which the middle strings are fastened. The second group consists of the two pins that are farthest from the two middle pins (labeled A in Fig. 7-5). The two pins of the third group are closer to the middle pins (labeled B in Fig. 7-5).

The tuning of the unisons begins by tuning all the A pins. It can be seen that the tuning hammer moves from pin to pin in a zigzag pattern. The strip mute is removed entirely once all the A pins have been tuned; again be careful not to damage the dampers. The B pins are tuned next. This time the tuning hammer moves in a slightly smaller zigzag pattern. By keeping these patterns in mind, the tuner can always be sure the hammer is on the correct pin. It should be noted that when the strip mute is removed entirely, the strings of the B pins are being tuned to two open strings. If this presents a problem at first, the strip can be reinserted to silence all the strings attached to the A pins. Reinsert the strip carefully, in order not to disturb the tuning just done. After the strip has been removed for the last time, the tuning of the A strings should be rechecked.

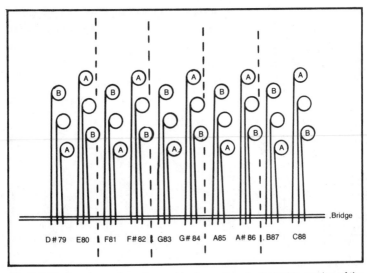

Fig. 7-5. Tuning pin configuration and tuning pattern in the treble section of the piano.

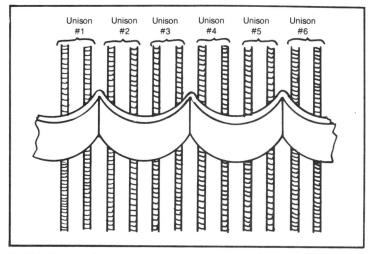

Fig. 7-6. Using a strip mute to silence one string in each of a series of bass unison groups.

The strip mute can also be used when tuning the bass, where there are two strings for each note. The strip is inserted between every other group of two strings (Fig. 7-6). First, the one open string is tuned, for each note is tuned to the one that is an octave higher. A zigzag pattern of pins to be tuned will become apparent upon inspection. The specific size and shape of the pattern will depend upon the configuration of the tuning pins. The bass notes are tuned, one string at this time, until the single string notes are reached. The tuning continues to the lowest note of the piano. The strip mute is then removed, and each untuned string is tuned to its unison mate.

FINISHING THE TUNING

The last step of tuning the piano involves tuning the unison strings in the tenor section. This can be done by tuning the outside strings to the middle strings with the temperament strip, as was done in the treble. The alternative is to use a rubber mute and move it from note to note, tuning first one unison string and then the other.

There is no right or wrong way to mute the piano for tuning. The student should experiment with the methods discussed here and use the one that seems the most comfortable both physically and psychologically. Some tuners prefer to mute the entire piano with strip mutes before beginning to tune; others use the strip mute only for the temperament octave and use mutes for the rest of the piano. Each person should use whatever method seems fastest and easiest.

Once the mutes have all been removed and the tuning completed, it is wise to go back over the piano and check for any mistakes, or notes that may have slipped. The tuning can be checked first by octaves and then by Fifths and Fourths. All of these intervals should be free of any fast beating. The beat speeds of the Major Sixths can also be checked. Remember that they should be faster the higher they are in the scale. A slow increase in their beat speeds while playing ascending Major Sixths, combined with smooth octaves, Fifths, and Fourths will confirm that the tuner has done a good job.

TESTS FOR ACCURACY

The importance of using tests to check the accuracy of tuning cannot be overstated. An octave may sound as if it has been tuned pure whereas it may really be slightly flat or sharp. This small amount of error can be enough to result in a poor tuning overall. Also, *inharmonicities* in the strings can require that some adjustments be made to the tuning of an octave. Tests tell the tuner when such adjustments are necessary and what changes are needed. For example, consider the tuning of C52 to C40. The octave may sound pure when it is tuned, and the Fifth F45-C52 may also sound pure whereas the Fourth G47-C52 may beat twice each second. This can be due to an inharmonicity in one of the strings. If so, the octave may have to be retuned so that the beating of the Fourth is not so objectionable. If the tuner does not check each note tuned, he will not be aware the problem exists. The following tests can be used to check the tuning of an octave.

Fifths and Fourths

When tuning up the scale, the Fifth and Fourth below the note tuned should be checked. When tuning down the scale, the Fifth and Fourth above the being tuned should be checked. In either case, these intervals should be close to pure. Neither should beat more often than once each second. Remembering that all Fifths should be slightly narrow of pure and all Fourths wide helps the tuner know how to change the octave to correct its tuning.

Minor Third-Major Sixth Test

This test is used by comparing the beat speeds of the minor

Third and Major Sixth that comprise the octave. The minor Third is taken from the lower note of the octave being tuned. Consider the octave C40-C52. The minor Third is C40-D#43, with D#43 being the test note. The Major Sixth is D#43-C52. When the octave has been correctly tuned, the beat speeds of both intervals should be identical. If the minor Third beats faster than the Major Sixth, then the octave is too narrow. If the minor Third beats slower than the Major Sixth, then the octave is too wide.

Major Third-Major Tenth Test

The Major Third below the lower note of the octave is used for this test. The speed of the beating of the Major Third is compared to the Major Tenth, which is comprised of the test note and the upper note of the octave. Consider the octave C40-C52 again as an example. The speed of the beating of the Major Tenth G#36-C52 should be the same as that of the Major Third G#36-C40, when the octave is pure. If the Major Third beats slower, the octave is too wide. If the Major Third beats faster, it is too narrow.

Major Third-Major Seventeenth Test

This is similar to the previous test, except that a double octave is used. For example, the tuning of C64 can be checked against C40 by using G#36 as the test note. The beat speed of the Major Third G#36-C40 should be the same as that of the Major Seventeenth G#36-C64. This test is especially helpful when tuning the higher parts of the treble section of the piano.

SPECIAL PROBLEMS

Several characteristics of pianos and piano strings can cause special problems for the person trying to tune the instrument. These include false beats, tuning in the extremely high treble and extremely low bass, string inharmonicities, and raising pitch.

False Beats

This is a phenomenon in which one string beats when played alone. It can be caused by rust on the string, by irregularities in string diameter or mass, and by other factors. It causes a problem to the tuner because it is difficult to distinguish between the beating of an interval and the false beat of one of the strings. If only one of the strings of the interval is beating, it is sometimes possible to remember the speed of the false beat and then tune the interval until it beats at that speed. This is the best that can be done because the false beat will always make the interval sound as if it is beating. When both strings have a false beat, tuning becomes even more difficult, and the tuner simply has to exercise his own judgment and tune for the sound that seems best, or least objectionable.

Tuning in the High Treble

Tuning in the high treble becomes difficult because of the short length of the strings. The upper harmonics are either nonexistent or so quiet that they cannot be used. Also, false beats are most common in this part of the piano. When approaching the extreme treble, it is sometimes helpful to tune to the note two octaves lower, instead of one octave lower. Eventually, the tuner has to rely on his sense of pitch because no beating will be distinguishable.

To help check the accuracy of high treble tuning, the tuner may play an arpeggio beginning an octave or two below the note being tuned. Playing an arpeggio means playing the notes of a chord in quick succession. For playing an arpeggio as a test, the chord starts with the lowest note in the octave, called the tonic. The other notes are a Major Third above the tonic, a Fifth above the tonic, and the highest note of the octave. Beginning with C40 for example, the notes in the chord are C40, E44, G47, and C52. An arpeggio is played by striking these keys one after the other. As the tuner plays the arpeggio, he should listen to see if the chord sounds pleasant and if the intervals seem properly spaced.

Another way to check the pitch of a high treble note is to start several octaves lower and play by octaves up the scale until the note being tuned is reached. Playing up a *chromatic scale* to the note being tuned may help by comparing the spacing in pitch between the semi-tones. A chromatic scale is one that uses every half step and, therefore, consists of 12 half steps to an octave.

In the end, each tuner devises his own way of determining if the high treble notes are at the correct pitch. The human ear tends to hear high notes as being lower than they really are. As a result, most tuners, if they err, tend to pull the treble notes too sharp. Keeping this in mind, and developing a good sense of pitch reference, will minimize problems with tuning in the high treble.

String Inharmonicities

To say that a string has inharmonicities means that one or more of its harmonics is not at the frequency that mathematics indicates it should be. Stiffness of piano wire is one of the main reasons for inharmonicity in the piano. It only causes a problem for the tuner when one of the harmonics in a note's series is drastically different from what it should be. This will result in a string that sounds generally well tuned, except that one harmonic may beat against a coincidental harmonic of some other note. In practice, this may show up when tuning an interval. It may seem impossible to eliminate the beating completely. Usually this is because the two notes of the interval may have a very high pair of coincidental harmonics that beats even when the lower harmonics are properly tuned. Concentrating on the lower harmonics and selectively ignoring the higher coincidentals will help eliminate any confusion. This type of problem is especially noticeable in the bass because the higher harmonics are more easily heard. Also they tend to be inharmonic because of the added stiffness caused by the copper windings.

Longitudinal Vibrations of Strings

The sound of the piano is produced by the strings vibrating back and forth. When a piano string is struck by the hammer, it vibrates not only back and forth, but also stretches along its length. This type of vibration is called the *longitudinal vibration* of the string. It produces a sound that is normally very quiet but that becomes loud enough in the bass to present a problem. The frequency of the sound produced by the longitudinal vibration is inherent in the scale design of the piano and cannot be changed by the tuner. If this frequency clashes with that of the note being played, it will create a dissonance that can be disconcerting to the tuner. These longitudinal vibration noises can become loud enough to make accurate tuning in the bass impossible. In general, the shorter the piano, the more of a problem this will be. The tuner can do nothing to compensate, so he must use his best judgment when tuning.

Tuning in the Low Bass

Besides inharmonicities and longitudinal vibrations, the bass notes can be difficult to tune simply because the fundamental harmonics of the lowest notes are of such low frequency. They approach the limits of human hearing and, in many cases, are overpowered by the upper harmonics. The tuner must concentrate very hard to pick out the lower harmonics. Sometimes, playing the upper note of an octave first, and then the lower one, makes it easier to hear the fundamental than if both are played simultaneously. The same techniques that are helpful in the high treble are useful in the low bass as well. Two additional tests will be of assistance in bass tuning.

One of these is to simply play descending Major Sixths. The beating of the Major Sixths is slow enough to count easily in the bass. The beat speeds should slow progressively when decending Major Sixths are played. A regular decrease in the speed of the beating indicates that the octaves are properly tuned. The other test is a variation of the Major Third-Major Seventeenth test. The test note is a seventeenth above the note being tuned. The other interval used in the test is made of the test note and the note two octaves above the one being tuned. For example, when tuning C4, the intervals used are C4-E32 and C28-E32. Both should beat at the same speed when C4 is properly tuned.

The tuner, however, may have to use his judgment in this part of the piano. Even though the tests may indicate that the note is tuned correctly, the note may not sound right because of inharmonicities. In such cases, the tuner must rely on his sense of pitch and tune the low bass notes to the pitch that sounds best, even though the tests may indicate it is not correct.

Raising Pitch

If the piano to be tuned is more than a quarter step low overall, a special tuning problem arises. If the tuner attempts to tune the piano to standard pitch, the tuning will not stabilize, and it will go out of tune quickly. If too much tension is added to a piano wire at any one time, the metal of the wire will relax, causing a drop in pitch. If this happens throughout the piano, it will end up going flat shortly after being tuned. At times, the piano may even sound worse after the tuning than it did before.

This problem can be avoided by performing an operation known as a pitch raise. This is done by first doing a very rough tuning. The idea is not to tune the piano, but to get the tension on the strings close to what it should be. The piano should then be allowed to stand for a few days and then be retuned. The second tuning should stabilize quite well. If the piano was very low to begin with, it may be necessary to do two rough tunings before attempting the final one. This step can be minimized by setting the rough tuning four or five cycles per second sharp of standard pitch. After the rough tuning of a pitch raise, a piano will fall in pitch at least four or five cycles per second. It may fall by as much as a half step, especially in the treble. By setting the rough tuning sharp, the piano tuner will have the piano closer to standard pitch upon returning to do the final tuning.

Care must be taken when doing the initial rough tuning to distribute the increased tension evenly, especially if the piano is old or very low in pitch. Tuning a piano that was originally a half step low to standard pitch adds about 5,000 pounds of stress to its frame. If the piano were tuned in the normal fashion, extreme stress would be added to the treble before any was added to the bass. This uneven distribution of stress could result in the plate's breaking if it had a small crack or structural flaw. If the piano is to be brought up a half step or more, it is best to tune just one string of each A first, followed by one string of each A#, B, and so on when doing the rough tuning. This will distribute the increased stress evenly, reducing the chances of damaging the plate. Once one string of each note has been roughly brought up to the correct tension, those remaining can be tuned. Again, it is best to do this in a way that distributes the tension evenly.

Lowering the pitch of a piano that has been left too high can create a problem the reverse of that encountered when raising pitch. The piano will tend to go sharp after tuning. Again, two tunings may be necessary, following the same general procedure used for raising pitch.

Chapter 8

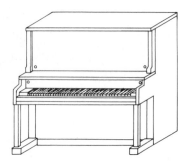

The Vertical Piano Action

The piano action is the physical link between the keys and the strings. It is basically a system of levers. Through the motion of these levers, the hammer is thrown forward against the strings whenever the key is struck. The action is also involved in damping the sound of the strings once the key has been released. The three types of vertical actions differ only in their locations vertically, relative to the keyboard. The upright action, found in the large, old upright pianos, sometimes called upright grands or cabinet grands, sits above the keys and is connected to them by a piece of wood called the sticker or abstract. This action is shown in Fig. 8-1.

In some upright pianos, the sticker is absent. It has been replaced by a long capstan made of dowel. Figure 8-2 shows the keyframe assembly and a key having a dowel capstan.

The direct blow action shown in Fig. 8-3, has the same parts as the upright action, although they may be somewhat smaller. This action functions in the same manner as the upright action, but the sticker is absent, and the action sits directly on top of the keys. The top action is functionally the same as the other two, but it sits below the level of the keys (Fig. 8-4). The key is connected to the action by a sticker made of wire or, occasionally, of wood. It is often called a drop lifter.

The operating principles of all three actions are the same. The explanation of how the vertical action works will be limited to the direct blow action. The only difference between it and the others is

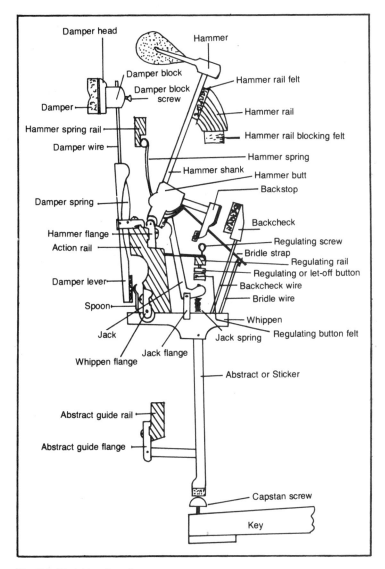

Fig. 8-1. Upright action diagram.

the absence of the sticker. The sticker merely acts as a connecting link between the key and the action and does not alter the functioning of the action. When studying these actions, keep in mind that it is a system of levers and that levers are used to change either the direction of a force or the amount of force on an object located at the other end.

107

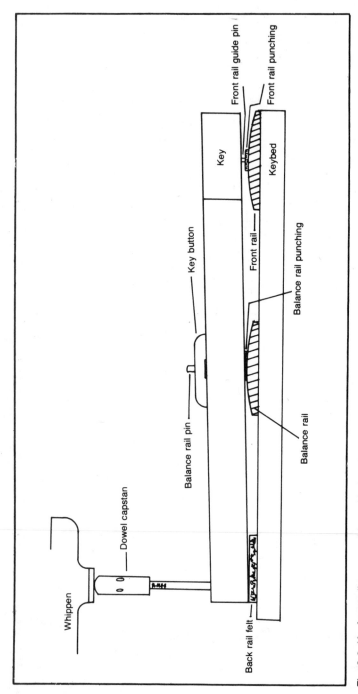

Fig. 8-2. Keyframe diagram and key with dowel capstan.

Whippen

Dowel capstan

Balance rail pin

Key button

Key

Front rail guide pin

Front rail punching

Keybed

Front rail

Balance rail punching

Balance rail

Back rail felt

108

Understanding that the action is a machine and understanding how that machine works enable the piano technician to isolate any problems in the mechanism and rectify them. Two types of action problems confront the piano technician. One concerns the *regulation* of the piano. Regulation is the adjustment of the various moving parts so that each works properly and at the proper time. The other problem concerns the repairs of broken parts. Regulating the action of a note is often necessary after doing some repair to the action parts of that note. For that reason, regulation of the action will be covered first.

OPERATION OF THE VERTICAL PIANO ACTION

When the front of the key is pushed downward, the back of the key rises, and the *capstan* lifts the *whippen*. The force of the moving

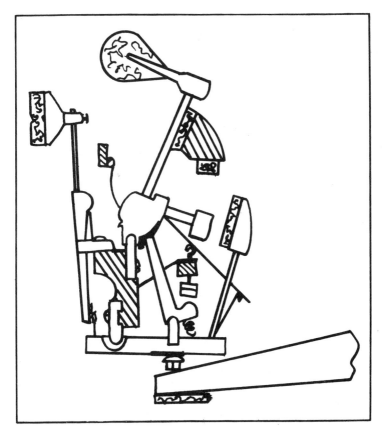

Fig. 8-3. Direct blow action diagram.

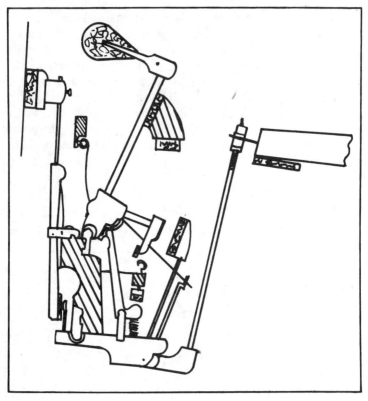

Fig. 8-4. Drop action diagram.

whippen is applied in two different directions. The *damper spoon*, on the back of the whippen pushes on the *damper lever*, lifting the *damper head* off the string. The *jack*, located on the front of the whippen, pushes upward on the *hammer butt*. This causes the hammer to swing forward toward the string. The motion of the jack would eventually force the hammer against the string, blocking it there, except for the let-off button. As the whippen (and the jack with it) rises, the heel of the jack hits the let-off button. This impact causes the top of the jack to swing out from under the hammer butt. Once this happens, the hammer may travel freely to the string, carried by its own momentum. Having hit the string, the hammer rebounds and is caught by the *backcheck*. As long as the key is still depressed, the backcheck holds the hammer by the *backstop*, and the damper remains lifted off the string.

Once the front of the key is let up, the whippen begins to drop. At this time, the backcheck releases the hammer, and it is pushed back against the *hammer rail* by the force of the *hammer spring*. As the whippen continues downward, the damper spoon moves backward toward the pianist, and the damper spring forces the damper against the string, stopping the sound. The note cannot be played again until the whippen has dropped far enough that the jack can return to its resting place under the hammer butt. The jack spring pushes the jack back to this location.

All this activity takes place in a fraction of a second as the key is played and released. If the parts are not correctly adjusted, the piano will not function properly or, perhaps, not at all. This is the purpose of regulating the action. Regulating involves adjusting the rest positions of the parts and making sure they move when they should.

REMOVING THE VERTICAL ACTION

It is often necessary to remove the piano action in order to make repairs, and it is sometimes necessary when regulating the action. Before attempting to remove the action, all the vertical trapwork dowels should be removed. On upright and direct blow actions, the bracket bolts or screws are removed. The top of the action is pulled back, tilting the action toward the technician, and so pulling the dampers off the strings. The action can be grasped with the fingers under the hammer rail and hooked into the action brackets. The thumbs are placed over the top of the hammer rail, keeping it in position against the brackets (Fig. 8-5). With the action still tilted, it can be lifted up and out of the piano.

Care should be taken not to catch the dampers on the bracket bolts, as this may damage the felt. With upright actions, some care must also be taken not to catch the bottoms of the *stickers* on the capstans or any case parts because they may break easily. Once the action is out of the piano, it should be placed where it cannot fall. It should not be leaned against any object so that the dampers are holding the weight of the action.

Drop actions require a bit more preparation before they can be removed from the piano. The Thayer action, which has the type of *inverted sticker* shown in Fig. 8-6, can be removed with no further preparation to the action. The keys may need to be removed in order to get enough clearance. The *sticker rail* is unfastened from its brackets and laid on top of the hammers. The action can then be removed in the same way as a direct blow.

The action shown in Fig. 8-4 will need to have the *drop lifter wires* disconnected from the ends of the keys. The wires will then

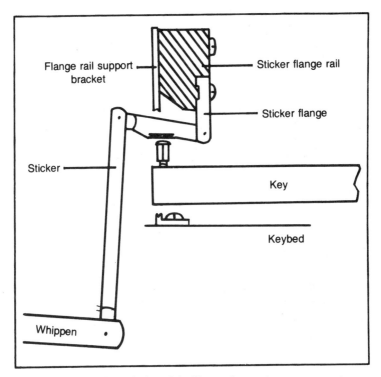

Fig. 8-6. Inverted sticker design of the Thayer drop action.

have to be secured to the hammer rail. This can be done with a long piece of thread or string. The string is fastened to one of the end action brackets. It is then looped around a group of 10 to 12 lifter wires before being wrapped around the hammer rail once or twice. Another group of wires is then gathered up and the string wrapped around the hammer rail again. Each time the string is wrapped around the hammer rail, it should be pulled tight so that the lifter wires are held against the hammer rail. Once all the wires are gathered up and held against the hammer rail by the string, it can be tied to the bracket at the other end of the action. Once the keys have been removed to give proper clearance, the action can be tilted away from the strings and then lifted up and out of the piano.

Depending on the design of the piano, the keys may or may not need to be removed in order to get enough clearance. Any time the keys are removed from the piano, they should first be numbered. The numbers can be written on each key between the key button and the capstan. This may not seem necessary since the numbers are often stamped on each key. These stamped numbers can be very

Fig. 8-7. Bracket hook of new Acrosonic action (photograph by Rich Strader).

difficult to read once the keys are out of the piano, if they get out of order. It is safer to number the keys before removing them.

REMOVING THE ACROSONIC DROP ACTIONS

There are two types of Baldwin Acrosonic drop actions. These need to be removed in a slightly different fashion from the action shown in Fig. 8-4 even though the whippen, hammer, and damper designs are basically the same. The main difference is in the design of the connection between the whippen and the key and in how these inverted stickers must be secured before the action is removed.

The new Acrosonic action looks very much like the one shown in Fig. 8-4, but near the bottom of each action bracket is a hook (Fig. 8-7). This hook is made to hold a 7/16″ dowel rod. A length of dowel, as long as the action, can be placed in these hooks. The dowel will then hold the lifter wires against the hammer rail. The action can then be removed without the time-consuming preparation of tying the wires to the hammer rail.

The inverted sticker design of the old Acrosonic action is shown in Fig. 8-8. In order to remove this action, the *pick up finger guide* rail must be fastened to several of the *pick up fingers*. When this is done, the guide rail can be lifted up, and it will still hold all the pick up fingers. If the rail comes off and releases all or part of the pick up fingers, it can be very difficult to get the fingers located properly again. Before unfastening the guide rail, one pick up finger at each end of the action and one in the middle should be raised to the rail and tied tightly so that they will be held in the position shown in

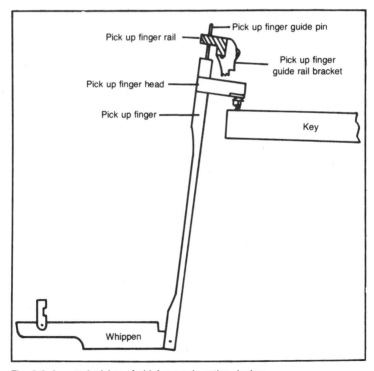

Fig. 8-8. Inverted sticker of old Acrosonic action design.

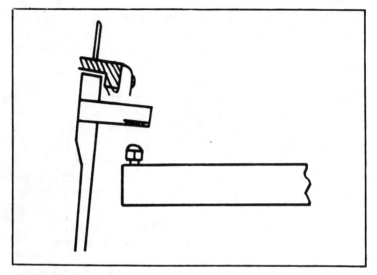

Fig. 8-9. Position of pickup finger when tied to guide rail before removing the old Acrosonic action.

Fig. 8-9. Once this is done, the guide rail can be unfastened from its brackets, and the action removed from the piano without danger of the pick up fingers coming out of their guide holes.

REGULATING THE VERTICAL ACTION

Before the actual task of regulating the piano begins, it is desirable to remove the action and keys in order to clean the piano. The action can be taken outside and the dirt blown from it by using a vacuum cleaner with the hose hooked to the exhaust. A small brush can be used to dislodge dust and dirt so that the air from the vacuum can blow it away. The area under the keys, as well as the area at the bottom of the piano, by the trapwork, should be cleaned. It is also a good idea to get behind the piano to remove any debris from between the soundboard and the horizontal support. Foreign objects that have fallen here may rattle or buzz against the soundboard when it vibrates.

While the action is out of the piano, the condition of the *keyframe felts* should be examined. If these felts appear badly worn, or if they are not soft and resilient, they should be replaced. The thickness of the existing felt should be measured. Replacement felts should be the same size. Sometimes, the *front* and *balance rail punchings* are so badly worn it is impossible to tell how thick they were originally. If this situation exists, the technician must use the case parts as a guide to tell what thickness of punchings should be used.

The thickness of the balance rail felts controls the height of the keys above the keyframe. They should not be so thick that the bottoms of the keys show above the key slip or so thin that the key tops will hit on the key slip when the piano is played. Key height can range from 2⅜″ to 2⅝″. If the piano is a newer model, the correct height may be available from the manufacturer or from the *Piano Action Handbook*, published by the Piano Technicians Guild.

This is also the time to check the action carefully. All of the *flange* screws should be tightened so that the flanges will fit firmly against the action rails. All the jack flanges should be checked, and any loose ones should be reglued to the whippens. The following repairs, which will be covered in Chapter 9, should also be done now if necessary: replace the bridle straps, replace or repin worn or damaged flanges, replace the damper felts, and file and reshape the hammers.

After the action and keys have been replaced and the trapwork dowels have been reinstalled, the regulation can begin. Regulation of the vertical action involves the following steps:

- Set the hammer blow distance.
- Space the hammers to fit the strings.
- Ease the keys.
- Level the keys.
- Space the keys.
- Eliminate lost motion.
- Set the key dip of the natural (white) keys.
- Regulate the let-off.
- Regulate the backchecks.
- Set the dip of the sharps.
- Regulate the dampers.
- Regulate the damper spoons.
- Adjust the bridle strap wires.

Setting the Hammer Blow Distance

The hammer blow distance is the distance between the hammers and the strings when the hammers are at rest on the hammer rail. Old uprights should have a blow distance of 1⅞″. The *Piano Action Handbook* will have the correct specifications for newer models. You may also consult the manufacturer. The blow distance is adjusted by adding or removing felt from the hammer rail blocking felt, also called the hammer rail rest pad. If the hammers are too far

Fig. 8-10. Adjusting the blow distance (photograph by Rich Strader).

from the strings, which is the usual case, a thin piece of felt should be glued to the bottom of the blocking felt (Fig. 8-10). Glue should be used very sparingly here because excess glue will harden the felt. This will cause the rail to make a noise when the soft pedal is used. If the hammers are too close to the strings, a thin layer of felt will have to be removed from the bottom of the blocking felt.

Spacing the Hammers

The hammers should strike all three strings squarely. To check this movement the hammers are first *traveled*. This is done by slipping the shank of a long screwdriver behind the shanks of 10 or more hammers. The hammers are then pushed forward simultaneously by the screwdriver. All of the hammers should travel in a straight line toward the strings. If one of the hammers wanders off to one side, it might be adjusted with traveling paper. A thin strip of paper, 1/16″ to ⅛″ wide, should be cut. It should be several inches long. The traveling paper is inserted under the flange of the offending hammer (Fig. 8-11). The traveling paper is inserted under the side of the flange opposite the direction that the hammer wanders.

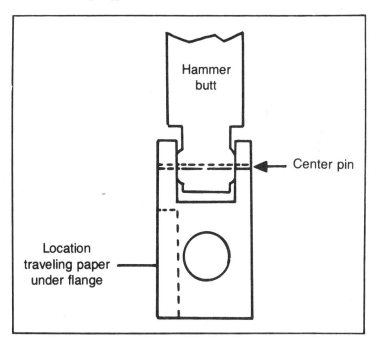

Fig. 8-11. Front view of a hammer flange showing location of traveling paper used to correct a hammer that drifts to the right.

A medium grit sandpaper, such as 220 grit, works well for traveling paper. The grit side should be placed against the flange. The glue that holds the sand particles in place will eventually glue the paper to the flange. The traveling paper should come off with the flange in the event that the flange should ever have to be replaced.

If a hammer travels properly, in a straight line to the strings, but is crooked and hits the strings at an angle, it can be made square by a process called *burning the shank*. The shank is not actually burned, but is heated with an alcohol lamp or butane lighter. Once the shank has been heated, the front of the hammer is twisted toward the side of the interference (Fig. 8-12). The hammer, once it is parallel to the others, is then spaced back so that it is in front of the strings.

If the hammer travels in a straight line and hits the string squarely, but off to one side, it will need to be repositioned. This is done by loosening the flange screw and moving the hammer to the desired position. The screw can then be tightened while holding the hammer in place. If the hammer is not held securely, it will move to the right when the screw is tightened.

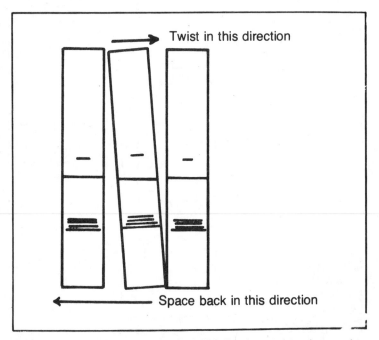

Fig. 8-12. Top view of hammers showing which direction to twist and space when burning the shank.

Easing the Keys

The fronts of the keys should be lifted up ¼″ and then released. If the key does not fall freely back into place, it is too tight at the *balance rail pin* and the *balance pin* hole in the key will need to be enlarged. A tool to do this can be made from a balance rail pin. The pin should be laid on an anvil and pounded with a hammer until it is flattened into a slightly elliptical shape. The pin is then fitted into a handle or held in a pliers. It is inserted into the balance pin hole and twisted gently to enlarge the hole. The end grain of the wood of the key is at the front and back of the hole, and it should not be enlarged in this direction. Instead, the tool should be inserted so that it compressed the wood only at the sides of the holes. Care must be taken not to enlarge the hole too much, or the key will wobble from side to side and rattle.

If the key fits properly at the balance rail pin, but binds when it is depressed, the front and balance *mortises* must be checked. The mortises can be enlarged with key easing pliers. The pliers must be squeezed hard enough to compress the wood at the sides of the mortise. If only the felt is compressed, it will spring back to its original dimensions later, causing the key to bind once more.

If the balance pin hole and the mortises seem free, but the key still sticks down, it may be rubbing against an adjacent key or against the *key slip*. If the key is rubbing against one of its neighbors, it can be removed and sanded on that side until there is enough clearance for the key to work freely. If the key rubs against the key slip, the slip will need to be moved away from the keys. If the key slip screws are loosened, a veneer shim can be put between the bottom of the key slip and the keybed. This will hold the slip farther away from the keys. Some pianos have a screw that holds the key slip away from the keys. If the slip is removed, the screw can be backed out part of a turn and the slip refitted. If the screw is backed out far enough, there will be enough clearance for the key to operate freely.

Occasionally a key may stick because of a misaligned guide rail pin. If the pin is so far forward or backward that it rubs against the front or back of the mortise, the key can bind. Sometimes the pin can be bent so that it will not rub against the mortise. If this does not work, the pin will have to be repositioned.

Leveling the Keys

The keys should be leveled so that they have a neat and uniform appearance. They should be set at a high enough level that the key

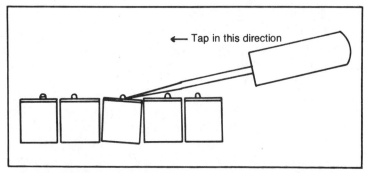

Fig. 8-13. Bending the balance rail pin with a screwdriver in order to level a key.

has room for sufficient downward travel. If there is not enough room for the key to travel, the action may not go through its full cycle. The height at which the keys should be leveled is variable. It is variable and can be changed somewhat to accommodate a particular piano.

Before the key height is set, the keys should all be set so that their tops are horizontal. If a key is cocked to one side (Fig. 8-13), the balance pin can be bent in order to straighten it. Without removing the key, a screwdriver is placed against the top of the balance pin and tapped until the key is properly aligned. If the fronts of the keys are not even, the balance pin can be bent front to back in the same manner in order to make the front surfaces even.

Once the keys are all square to the key slip, the process of setting the key height can begin. This is done by adding or removing paper and cardboard punchings at the balance pin. The height of one white key at the end of each section should be set with a ruler. Once these samples are properly leveled, the remaining white keys are set to them. A straightedge is used to bridge between the sample keys in order to check the level of the others.

Once the naturals have been leveled, the sharps are leveled so that they are ½″ above the tops of the white keys. Again, sample keys can be set, and a straightedge can be used to check the height of the remaining keys.

Whenever placing paper or cardboard punchings on the balance pins, first lay the paper or cardboard on top of the felt punching in order to facilitate removing any excess. Later, after all the keys have been leveled, the felt and paper punchings should be grasped as a unit and turned over so that the felt is on top. If this is not done, the key will make a noise when it rubs or hits against the paper or cardboard. This same procedure is also used later when setting the dip of the keys by placing punchings on the guide rail pins.

Spacing the Keys

A *key spacer* is used to move the fronts of the keys from side to side. It is inserted under the front rail punchings and is used to bend the guide pin slightly. The key spacer is put under the punching in order to avoid scratching the pin where it can rub and abrade the felt in the key mortise. This would cause excessive wear of the key felts.

Eliminating Lost Motion

The lost motion to be eliminated is the amount of movement of the jack before it contacts the hammer butt. The clearance between the top of the jack and the butt should be about 0.003″. In practice, there should be just enough clearance that the jack will reset under the hammer butt when the key is released very slowly. Lost motion is adjusted by turning the capstan screws. Two types of capstan wrenches are used for this. One is used with capstans that have a square section of shank just above the threads. The other type of capstan has holes above the threads; the pointed wrench fits into these holes. The pointed capstan wrench is sometimes called a capstan screwdriver. Because the capstan is threaded, turning it raises or lowers its top surface. This in turn changes the height of the jack.

The lost motion can be checked by playing the key normally and then releasing it very slowly. The key is then struck with a sharp blow. If the jack was not able to reset, meaning not enough clearance, then it will skip out from under the butt, and the note will sound weak or will make no sound at all. If there is so much lost motion that the key feels sloppy, the piano will lose power and dynamic range.

Setting the Key Dip of the Naturals

The *dip* is the amount of downward motion of the key. Most vertical pianos require a dip of ⅜″. A *key dip block* can be used to check this, provided the keys have been properly leveled. The dip block is put on top of the key to be checked, and then the key is depressed. The top of the block should be level with the tops of the adjacent keys. Dip is adjusted by adding or removing paper and cardboard punchings at the front rail. The amount of downward pressure on the key will affect the dip when making this adjustment. Because the felt punchings under the fronts of the keys will compress with a heavy touch, it is necessary to use the same force when pushing down on the keys to check dip. One pound of pressure is the desired amount to use.

The dip of the naturals may be set first by using the key dip block to regulate all the C's and F's. The rest of the keys are set to these. When setting them, a finger is used to feel across the tops of the keys to see if they are at the same height when depressed. This process is referred to as *drumming off*, and again it is very important to use uniform pressure on the keys that are being pushed down.

Regulating the Let-Off

This adjustment is concerned with how close the hammer comes to the strings before the escapement mechanism operates and the hammer is carried forward only by its own momentum. The jack should slip out from under the hammer butt when the hammer is ⅛″ from the strings. When this happens, the hammer has escaped from the influence of the key and whippen. Test let-off by depressing the key very slowly. The hammer will travel toward the strings until the point of escapement, and then it will fall back. Measure the distance of the hammer from the strings when the hammer just begins to fall back. If it is not ⅛″, the let-off will need to be adjusted by turning the regulating screw, which will raise or lower the regulating button. Turning the screw clockwise will lower the button, causing escapement to happen when the hammer is farther from the strings. The regulating screwdriver is made especially to slip over the regulating screw.

Regulating the Backchecks

The backchecks are adjusted by bending the backcheck wires with the tool made for this purpose. When using the backcheck regulating tool, care must be taken not to twist or bend the wire with such force that the whippen is cracked. The whippen should be held firmly while bending the wire in order to avoid damage at the center pin. If the whippen is not secured while bending the wire, the flange bushing or the wood around it may be damaged. This would cause the whippen to wobble and make noise. The backchecks must first be aligned so that they are directly behind the backstops. The catching surfaces of both parts should be parallel so that they meet squarely.

The backchecks of one natural key near the end of each section are then adjusted by bending the wire front to back. The hammer should be held ⅝″ from the strings when checked after a moderate blow to the key. These samples will be used as a guide for adjusting the remaining backchecks. The strength of the blow used when adjusting these notes will determine to some extent how far the hammer checks from the strings, so the blows used when regulating the samples will need to be uniform.

Keep in mind that when a backcheck is bent forward, the holding surfaces of it and the backstop will no longer be parallel. To keep them parallel, the wire should be bent near the whippen initially to move the backcheck closer to the backstop. Another bend, in the opposite direction, is then made near the backcheck itself (Fig. 8-14). This second bend returns the two parts to the desired parallel position. This principle of double bending also applies when the backcheck is moved from side to side because the backchecks and backstops should be aligned squarely in all respects.

Once the backchecks near the end of each section have been regulated, a straightedge is used to bridge across these samples. The rest of the backchecks are lined up with the straightedge. The backchecks must be lined up accurately because their positions will be used to regulate the dip of the sharp keys.

Setting the Dip of the Sharps

The dip of the sharps is regulated by striking two natural keys with one hand and the sharp between them with the other. The blows used on the keys must be uniform in strength. When the dip of the sharp is correct, the checking distance of the hammers from the strings should be identical. Add or remove punchings under the front of the sharp until it checks at the same distance as the naturals. If the keys have been properly leveled, and the backchecks lined up accurately, the dip of the sharps will be correct when all the

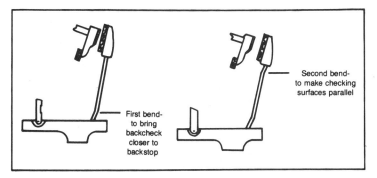

Fig. 8-14. Double bending of a backcheck wire in order to keep the checking surfaces parallel.

hammers check at a uniform distance from the strings. If the backchecks are badly worn in one area of the keyboard, it may be necessary to measure the dip of the sharps. The dip should be ⅜″ at the front of the key.

Regulating the Dampers

Before the dampers are regulated, the *damper lifter rods* should be adjusted. The *damper pedal* and the *bass sustain pedal* should move only ⅛″ at the tip before the damper lifter rod begins to move. Adjusting the lost motion of the pedals is done by adjusting the *horizontal trapwork rod*. This is adjusted near the pedal by screwing the nut up and down on the bolt that runs up from the back of the pedal. On some older pianos, the horizontal rod is made of metal and fits into a hole in the back end of the pedal. A bolt through the pedal holds the rod in place. To adjust the lost motion, the bolt is loosened. The rod is then repositioned and the bolt tightened. When adjusting the damper pedals, it is a good idea to adjust the soft pedal as well. There should be no lost motion of the damper pedal. The hammer rail should begin to rise as soon as the soft pedal is depressed.

Once the lifter rods are adjusted properly, depress the damper slowly and watch the motion of the dampers. They should lift off the strings at the same time. If the dampers at one end of the piano lift early, one of the lifter rod hooks is bent. The action must be taken out of the piano and the lifter rod removed. The bent hook must then be bent back to the proper position so that the dampers will all lift at the same time. The proper amount of bending can be checked only by reinstalling the lifter rod and putting the action back into the piano. Then the pedal can be depressed and the action of the dampers observed once more.

If individual dampers lift early or late, the damper wires must be bent forward or backward just above the top of the damper lever. A counterbend must then be made just below the damper block so that the damper will rest flat on the strings. The damper wires may need to be bent side to side if one of the strings is not being damped effectively because the damper is not lined up with the strings. The damper regulating tool is used to bend the wires. It is sometimes advantageous to work with two damper regulators at the same time. One is used just above the top of the lever; the other, just below the block. The slots in the damper regulating tools are cut at different angles relative to the handle. This facilitates making bends in different directions, regardless of the orientation of the wire or the location of the damper in the piano. It is a good idea, therefore, to have several of these tools with slots cut at various angles.

Regulating the Damper Spoons

The damper spoons are adjusted with the *spoon bender*. The shank of the spoon is bent backward and forward to affect the timing of the damper lift when the key is played. This takes some practice because the spoon bender is inserted between the whippens and must catch on the desired spoon. All the time, the technician cannot see the spoon or the end of the bender as they are hidden by the other action parts. When buying a spoon bender, check to see that the slot cut to fit the spoon shank is large enough. Sometimes this slot is not large enough to catch on the spoon and must be widened before the tool can be used effectively. A long spoon bender is used on spinets because the level of the spoons is below the keybed. The longer tool allows the technician to work under the keybed and still reach the spoons.

The spoons should be adjusted so that the dampers begin to lift when the hammers are ⅝″ from the strings. Bending the spoon toward the strings makes the damper lift earlier. It takes only a small bend of the spoon to make a substantial change in the timing of the damper action.

Adjusting the Bridle Strap Wires

The *bridle straps* should be tight when the soft pedal is depressed. Step on the soft pedal and observe any movement of the backchecks. If a backcheck moves, the bridle strap is too taut. Bend the wire toward the strings. If the strap is too loose, bend the wires away from the strings. As a final check, observe all the straps while depressing the pedal and releasing it.

General Considerations

Regulating a piano is an art that requires patience and practice. A rushed job will result in a poor regulation. Care must be taken to make all measurements and adjustments accurately. The student should first try regulating a group of only a few notes in his piano until he is totally familiar with the operation of the action and the principles behind it. Once this has been done a total regulation should be tried. Regulating gets better and easier with practice, so the student should regulate as many pianos as possible when learning this craft.

Chapter 9

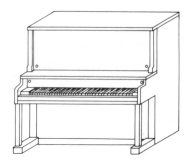

Repairing the Piano

Repairing the piano involves two phases. One is troubleshooting—locating the source of a malfunction. This would include finding the cause of extraneous noises and eliminating them. Successful troubleshooting depends on knowledge of the piano's construction and an understanding of its operating principles. It also requires that the problem be approached in a logical way that will isolate the cause of a problem. The other phase involves the actual repair or replacement of the piano's part. This chapter will include all the most common repairs, except those pertaining to hammers. Proper care of hammers will be discussed in Chapter 10.

TROUBLESHOOTING

When problems arise in the operation of the vertical piano action, the technician must be able to locate the source of the problem. Action problems may result in keys that stick or in notes that do not play or do not repeat properly. The first step in locating the source of the problem is to find out if it is originating in the keys or in the action. By pushing forward the backcatch, the whippen can be lifted off the key. The operation of the key can then be studied independently to see if it is functioning properly. If the key works freely, the technician knows the problem is in the action and can search for its cause by testing each part individually. When troubleshooting action problems, each part must be isolated for independent testing. If all the individual parts seem to work correctly, the interaction between the parts should then be checked. For example, keys that seem to stick before returning to the proper rest position are often the result of inadequate clearance between the jack and the hammer butt.

Action problems often turn out to be a matter of improper regulation. In this case, the technician has only to make a few adjustments to the offending notes, and the problem will be rectified. If the trouble turns out to be a broken, damaged, or poorly made part, the technician must repair or replace it.

A common source of complaints from piano owners is unusual sounds and noises coming from the piano. The technician must remember that there are no good, uniform words to describe sounds. What one person describes as a rattle, another may call a buzz, squeak, or clunk. The technician must then become something of a detective trying to ascertain which sound the customer is trying to describe. Many times, the customer is inquiring about a sound which is normal to piano operation, but was not heard until the piano was tuned or properly regulated. The technician must ask questions about the type of sound, how often it is heard, and when it is most often heard. Pianos will sometimes make noises on wet days, but not on dry days. Sometimes a sound is heard only when using one of the pedals or when playing loudly or softly. If the technician is not immediately sure what sound the piano owner is complaining about, he should ask many questions and try to piece together the puzzle of the most likely source of the sound. This is especially important with sounds that are only heard intermittently.

Unwanted and irritating noises associated with the piano can be grouped into five categories. These are string noises, case noises, external noises, action noises, and trapwork noises.

The most common source of noises from wound strings is due to the winding itself, which can come loose from the core wire. In such a case, the string should be loosened and removed from the hitch pin. The wire is then twisted a turn or two in the direction it is wound and reinstalled on the hitch pin. This twisting will effectively tighten the winding on the core wire and may eliminate the unwanted sound. If a wound string still makes noise after twisting, it will be necessary to replace the wire if a loose winding is thought to be the cause of the problem.

Other noises from strings arise from the points where they cross over the bridges. Often, the upper bridge and capo have rough spots that will cause the string to buzz if it vibrates against them. If the string is loosened slightly and moved laterally at the bridge, the problem may be solved. The lower bridge may also be a source of trouble if the string is not seated firmly on it, but is riding above it. The blade of a screwdriver can be placed on the string, near the bridge pin, and the string tapped down until it is tight against the bridge.

The lower bridge pins may also be a source of noise that will appear to be caused by the strings. The bridge pins may be loose because of small cracks in the bridge. Small cracks may be repaired by removing the bridge pin and putting a small amount of epoxy into the hole. The pin is reinserted and heated with a soldering iron, which will cause the epoxy to flow into the cracks. A string may also buzz against a bridge pin if the pin has not been properly aligned so that the string has enough side bearing on it. The pins should be staggered so that the strings zigzag over the bridge (Fig. 9-1). If the pins are not aligned properly, the string will have too little side bearing on the pin and will make noise (Fig. 9-2). If the location of the pin is only slightly wrong, it can be bent to one side by placing a screwdriver blade against the side of the pin. Using the screwdriver

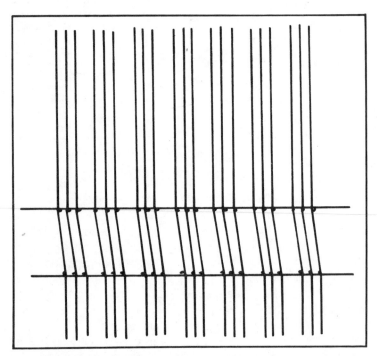

Fig. 9-1. Correct bridge pin configuration.

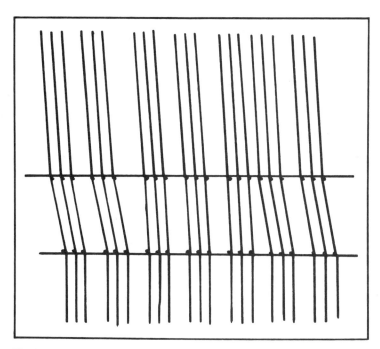

Fig. 9-2. Improperly aligned bridge pins.

like a punch, the technician can bend the pin by tapping the screw-driver with the heel of the hand.

If the bridge pin is badly out of position, it will be necessary to remove it. The hole should be plugged by a piece of maple, and a new hole should be drilled in the proper location. The correct location for the new hole can be found by stretching a length of string or thread from the tuning pin to the hitch pin. The string will bisect the proper location for the pin holes.

Deciding whether a particular noise is caused by strings can be difficult. When one note alone seems to be causing the offending sound, an attempt should be made to discover which string of the unison group seems to be causing the problem. This can be done by muting all but one string at a time with rubber mutes. If the noise seems to come from all three strings, it is likely its source is somewhere other than the strings. Likewise, if sound is caused by several notes, its cause is likely to be other than strings. There are no hard and fast rules, though, so all possible sources of the noise must be considered until the problem is solved.

Parts of the piano case will often vibrate sympathetically when one or more notes of the piano are played. These parts will often cause a buzzing or rattling sound that will be mistaken for string-related noises. A common source of case noises is foreign objects that have fallen behind the piano and are caught between the soundboard and the horizontal support. When the soundboard vibrates, it rattles when it touches the object. The hardware that holds lids, fronts, and fallboards is also a common source of noise. The technician may need to have another person play the notes that cause the problem while he moves around the piano, holding on to various parts when attempting to find the source of a noise.

A sound that appears to be caused by a string or case part may be due to the sympathetic vibration of an object not related to the piano at all. Picture frames, mirrors, light fixtures, piano lamps, and even furniture may rattle when the piano is played. Sometimes the sound may even appear to be originating from within the piano.

Noises in the action are most often caused by damaged parts and will cause a clicking sound. Isolating the action parts for testing will help locate the source of the sound. Missing hammer butt felts, flanges that are not screwed tightly to the action rail, worn flange bushings, and hammers that are not glued to their shanks are common sources of trouble. Backstops and jacks should be checked to make sure they are glued tightly in place. Loose key tops will also make noise. Excess glue that has fallen into the action during manufacture may be struck by one of the moving parts, making a clicking or squeaking noise. Springs may rub against wood parts because of worn bushings or improper installation. Dirty or corroded center pins are a frequent cause of squeaks. Under no circumstances should they be treated with oil or other lubricants because they will get gummy and ruin the action. Center pins should be replaced if they are encrusted with dirt or if the bushing felt is hardened with age.

The pedals of the piano may squeak in the pedal mounts. A mixture of petroleum jelly and talc can be used to eliminate these noises. The trapwork is the only part of the piano that can be treated with petroleum lubricants. Silicone spray can often be used successfully, but great care must be taken not to get the lubricant on the strings. Silicone will travel up the strings and work its way into the pinblock, ruining the ability of the piano to stay in tune. Noises may also be caused by trapwork pieces rubbing together. Wood parts may be sanded to provide clearance, or the brackets that hold the parts may need to be relocated slightly.

A squeak that seems to be caused by the sustain pedal may actually be found to be originating from the damper lifter rod. This rod will often squeak at its hangers, where it is fastened to the action rail. The rod will need to be removed and a petroleum jelly/talc lubricant applied. Silicone may be used if care is taken to keep it off the strings. If necessary new felts should be installed.

COMMON REPAIRS

The most common problems the technician is likely to find, and the proper ways to eliminate the trouble, are listed below. Even though most damaged parts can be repaired, the repair sometimes requires large amounts of time. It is often cheaper for the customer simply to replace defective parts. The repairs that can be made should be learned, however, in case the technician is called upon to make a repair when replacement parts are not available.

Loose Key Bushing Felt

Bushing felt that has become loose or has fallen out will be noticeable because the key will wobble or will have a woody sound when the key is played. The key will need to be removed and the loose bushing felt reglued and wedged in place. Special wedges are sold by the technicians' supply companies. If the bushing is missing, a new one will have to be cut, then glued and wedged in place. After the glue has dried, the key is returned to the keyframe and checked to see if it works freely. The new bushing may need to be eased with key easing pliers, as described in Chapter 8.

Rebushing an entire set of keys is a time-consuming job, but it is the only solution if many of the keys wobble or rattle. The first step in rebushing a set of keys is to remove the old bushing felt. Number the keys and remove them from the keyframe. A group of 10 to 12 keys is placed on the workbench, and a damp cloth is laid over the key bushings. A hot iron can then be set on top of the cloth. The steam from the cloth will loosen the felts in a few minutes. The felts will be easy to remove with tweezers once the glue bond has been broken. This operation can be done quite quickly if one group of keys is being prepared while another is being steamed.

Once all the felts have been removed, the keys should be allowed to dry before new felts are installed. The new felts should have the same thickness, if it can be determined, as of the original felts. A strip of bushing felt 1-1½" long is laid over the top of the mortise, after a thin layer of glue has been applied to the edges of the mortise. The felt is then pushed down into the hole and cut with a razor blade or sharp knife. A wedge or clamp is then inserted to hold the bushing in place while the glue dries. The felt in the balance mortise must not be so long that it leaves a loose end of felt sticking down into the hole. If this happens, the balance rail pin will not fit freely through the balance pin hole and mortise. Once the glue in the mortise has dried, the excess felt that is sticking out of the hole is cut off flush with the key. After the keys are back on the keyframe, they will have to be checked to see if any need easing.

Loose Key Buttons

Loose key buttons will need to be reglued. Common household white glue is good for this type of repair. If a key button is missing or broken, it will need to be replaced. The new buttons come in a strip and will need to be cut to match the width of the key. The key will need to be on the keyframe when the new button is glued on so that the button may be centered. Once the glue has dried, the key button can be filed to make a smooth surface with the side of the key.

Loose Capstan Screws

Loose capstan screws will be found infrequently and will not normally require extensive repairs. Once the capstan has been removed, white glue and several small pieces of veneer can be put into the hole, and the capstan can be screwed back into place. The glue and veneer will make the hole small enough so that the screw should be tight.

Balance Pin Hole too Large

With many years of use, or careless removal of the keys by technicians, the balance pin holes may become enlarged. The key will move from front to back or wobble from side to side. The hole can be reduced to the correct dimensions by glue sizing. Sizing solution is made by adding one tablespoon of white glue to a quart of water. If a balance pin hole needs to be sized, the key should be removed and turned upside down. A measured amount of sizing can be applied by dipping a number 10 wood screw into the solution. The screw will pick up a small amount of the sizing solution, which can be applied to the hole. If too much sizing is applied and the hole becomes too small, it can be eased as described in Chapter 8.

Broken Keys

A broken key can be repaired by gluing the key together at the break and gluing a piece of veneer to either side of the break to act as a splint. The most common place for the key to break is at the balance pin hole because this is the key's weakest point. Care must be taken when gluing the two halves together to be sure the parts are correctly aligned. Otherwise, the hole will not be the correct size and shape. If the veneer splints cause the key to rub against adjacent keys, they can be sanded, once the glue has dried, to make proper clearance.

Loose Action Centers

The action centers are the pivots about which the action parts move. The action parts are hinged to flanges, which are bushed with felt. The flange and the moving action part are held together by a small pin called the *center pin*. When the flange bushing felt gets worn, the action part will begin to wobble. The action centers can become so worn that the felt is partially destroyed. The working of the action will also be affected by the pin's wobbling in the bird's-eye hole in the action part. The center pin should be held tightly by the unbushed bird's-eye, and should move within the bushed holes of the flange. Occasionally, a different type of flange will be found with the flange unbushed and the action part bushed. The principle is the same, and the pin should be held tightly by the unbushed holes.

In the event that an action center is found to be too loose, the only remedy is to repin the flange with a pin having a larger diameter. While it may be economically better simply to replace the flange with a new one, the technician should have the skill and ability to repair and rebush a flange. The pins that come with new flanges are often the wrong diameter to fit into the action part, and some adjustments will need to be made. These adjustments are the same as those used in the final steps of regulating a rebushed flange. This regulation is explained next.

Repinning a Flange

Once the problem flange has been removed from the piano, the center pin is removed. A special punch can be used to do this, or a smaller center pin held in pliers can be used to push out the old one. The diameter of the pin should be gauged, either with a center pin gauge or with a micrometer. The size of the old pin will help in determining the size of the new pin. If the old bushing has not been damaged, a new pin of a larger size may be used. It must be sufficiently larger so that it will be tight enough in the bushings.

First, the new pin should be checked for size with the hole in the action part. If the pin can be inserted through the hole with the fingers, it will be too small once the part and the flange are assembled. The pin should be large enough so that pliers will have to be used to insert the pin through the hole. If, on the other hand, the pin is too large, the wood of the action part may split. If the size of pin needed for a secure fit in the bushed flange is too large for the bird's-eye, that hole will have to be enlarged with a reamer. A reamer can be made by rolling a pin of the next smaller size between two files. Once the files have roughed up the surface of the pin, it can be used to enlarge the bird's-eye hole. An entire set of reamers of various sizes can be made in this way. Hammer shanks can be used as handles. Once the center pin has been found to fit tightly in the action part, it should be checked for fit in the flange. This is done by assembling the flange and action part and seeing how easily the parts swing.

Hammer flanges are the ones most frequently in need of repinning because the hammer moves through a larger arc than the other parts. To test a hammer flange, it is held vertically, and the hammer is moved to a horizontal position and then released. Count the number of times the hammer swings before it comes to rest. The hammer should swing from one side to the other five to seven times before stopping. If the hammer swings fewer times, the action center is too tight, and the bushing will need to be enlarged using a reamer made of a center pin. If the action center is still too loose, a larger size pin should be used. This may require additional reaming of the bird's-eye hole in the action part.

If the old bushings are found to be damaged, they should be removed and replaced with new ones. Figure 9-3 shows the steps in rebushing a flange. A strip of flange bushing felt approximately ¼″ wide is used. It is cut to a point on one end. As the point is started through one of the holes in the flange, it will roll up into a tube that will fill the hole. The point is pulled across the middle of the flange, started through the other hole, and pulled out the other side. The bushing felt should be pulled far enough so that none of the pointed part of the felt is inside the flange. A small amount of glue is then applied to the felt just beside the flange. The felt with the glue is then pulled inside the holes in the flange. A center pin of the size to be used should then be inserted into the felt tube. This pin will hold the felt tightly against the wood, ensuring a proper glue bond. After the glue has dried, the felt can be cut away at the edges of the flange after the pin has been removed. If the action center seems too tight after assembly, the bushing may have to be reamed to make a proper fit.

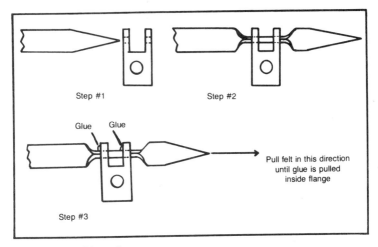

Step #1

Step #2

Glue   Glue

Pull felt in this direction
until glue is pulled
inside flange

Step #3

Fig. 9-3. Rebushing a flange.

Tight Action Centers

Tight action centers are caused most often by moisture being absorbed in the bushing felt. The moisture causes the felt to swell, which makes the fit on the center pin too tight. Tight centers can also be caused by a burr on the center pin, corrosion or dirt on the flange bushing felt, or an ill-fitting pin. If moisture is suspected as the reason for the tight center, the felt can be treated with a mixture made of 15 percent water and 85 percent methanol. A few flakes of good quality soap (not detergent) should be put into this mixture to act as a lubricant. Adding a higher percentage of water will increase the shrinking that occurs. A drop is put on each bushing. This will initially swell the bushing, making any binding worse, but as the mixture evaporates it will shrink the felt. A burred center pin, or an ill-fitting pin, will need to be replaced. Dirt or corrosion on the bushings can be cleaned by putting a drop of dry-cleaning fluid on the bushing felt.

Broken Hammer Shanks

If the shank has broken in the middle, the broken parts can be pulled from the hammer and butt by using a hammer head and butt extractor. If the break is near the butt, it will save time simply to replace the butt and the shank. If the break is near the hammer so that the extractor cannot be used, the broken shank will have to be drilled out. The angle of the new hole must match precisely the angle of the original, or the hammer will be held in the wrong position. Guide tools for boring the holes correctly are sold by piano technicians' supply companies.

If the shank has broken at an angle, it is often feasible to glue the two halves back together. Some method is needed to hold the two halves of the shank together. Heavy thread can be wound around a shank at the break until it completely covers the break, or special splints, sold by the supply companies, can also be used.

Broken Brass Butt Plates and Flanges

At one time, brass hammer butt plates were used either to secure the hammer to a regular wooden flange or to fasten the hammer to a brass *flange rail*. The flange rail is a strip of brass running the length of each section of the piano. The brass flange, which is a protruding extension of this rail, tends to break as the piano ages. Special clips have been made to repair these breaks. There are two types of clips. The place of the break determines which clip is used. Type A is used when the flange has broken at the groove. Type B is used if the break is at the hole. Types KA and KB are made especially to repair brass flanges in Kimball pianos.

New butt plates can be bought to replace any that are broken. It is necessary to remove the action to get to the screw that fastens the plate to the hammer butt or flange rail. Replacing a butt plate without something to hold it in place is very difficult. A special butt plate insert is made for this purpose. Forceps, available from a medical supply company, are handy for this and many other repairs. If no tool is available, the butt plates can be held in position by putting a small amount of rubber cement on the end of a finger. Once the cement has partially dried, the plate can be stuck to it.

Broken Hammer Springs

A replacement spring is made that can be installed without removing the action. A small hole is started in the hammer spring rail with an awl. The fastener at the end of the spring can then be screwed to the front of the spring rail. The hole for the screw should be positioned just above the end of the broken spring. If the spring coil is still attached to the rail, it may be necessary to remove the broken end. The broken end can simply be pulled from the rail with pliers.

Broken Damper Spring

Again, a special replacement spring is made for this repair, which can be made with the action in the piano. It is necessary first to loosen the damper flange screw. The hooked end of the replacement spring is placed under the loosened screw. Once the screw is tightened, the spring will be held securely in place, and the end of the spring can be put into place on the damper lever.

Broken Jack Springs

Replacement springs can be installed once the old spring has been removed and the glue reamed from the hole with the tool made for this purpose. It is normally necessary to remove the whippen from the action to do this. The spring is glued only to the whippen. The other end is held in place by a post in the hole under the bottom of the jack; it should not be glued.

Broken Bridle Straps

The bridle straps serve as the only connection between the hammer and the whippen and assist in the repetition of the piano action. With age, the fabric of the strap deteriorates and eventually breaks. There are three types of replacements.

Regular bridle straps can be tacked to the base of the backstop dowel, where it fastens to the hammer butt. This operation is difficult and time-consuming, so most technicians avoid this method. Alternately, the bridle strap can be glued into the hole in the backstop. A hammer shank with a pin in the end can be used to insert the strap into the hole, glue having been previously applied to the edges of the hole. Wait until the glue has dried completely before attaching the straps to the wires. The length of the strap can easily be adjusted to match that of the originals. Extreme adjusting of the bridle wires will not be necessary.

Bridle straps with cork fasteners can be easily and quickly attached by inserting the cork into the hole in the backstop. Again, a hammer shank with a pin in it works well as an inserter. Unless the cork fits very tightly in the hole, glue should also be used. The length of these straps cannot be adjusted, so the bridle wires may have to be bent severely for proper regulation of the piano.

Spring clip bridle straps can be used on pianos that have no hole in the backstop. The clips are attached to the backstop dowel. This can usually be done by hand, without the aid of a special tool. Some length adjustment of the strap can be made by wrapping it under the clip before it is fastened to the dowel, but this may cause the clip to fit poorly and come unhooked.

Broken Strings

The best way to repair a broken string is to replace it with a new one. The old wire should be removed and gauged so that a new wire of the same diameter and sufficient length can be cut. The new wire should be cut so that it will be long enough to reach from one tuning pin, down around the hitch pin, and back to the other tuning pin, with an extra 4″ on each side. When the new wire is installed, it will be wound around each tuning pin three times to form the coils. The extra 4″ on each side of the wire is the length that will be needed to make the three turns around the tuning pins.

In practice, the wire can be cut so that it will be quite a few inches longer than necessary. It can then be folded in half with a bend made at its mid-point. The ends of the wire are pushed under the capo and brought up past the tuning pins until the bend at the wire's mid-point is caught on the hitch pin. Each side of the wire can then be cut 4″ above its respective tuning pin. Before winding the wire on the tuning pins, remember that they will need to be backed out of the pinblock three full turns to allow room for the coils that will be made with the new wire.

When the wire is inserted in the hole in the tuning pin, it should be pushed in far enough so that it reaches through the pin and its end is flush with the other side. The end of the wire should not be pushed out the other side of the pin. Many manufacturers have adopted the practice of pushing the wire out the other side of the pin and then bending it back along the circumference of the pin. This makes installing the wire easier and quicker, but it results in sloppy looking work. It also makes a problem for the technician if the string should have to be replaced because the bent end can be hard to get out of the tuning pin.

After the string is inserted in the tuning pin, the pin is turned clockwise while holding a finger against the wire where it enters the pin. The wire will bend as the pin is turned and will follow along the pin to make the coil. The bend where the wire enters the pin is called the *becket*. The string should be wound neatly from the becket toward the back of the pin. Care must be taken to be sure the wire does not wind over itself at any point.

Once all three windings are in place with the string pulled fairly tight, they can be pulled forward to make a neat, tight coil. A special tool, a *string lifter,* is made for this purpose. It is a lever, which fits between the coil and the plate, that can be used to pry the coil forward. It cannot be used on many pianos because of insufficient room between the tuning pins, so a screwdriver may have to be used instead. The string lifter, or a screwdriver, may be needed to keep the string aligned when making the coil because the wire has a tendency to cross over upon itself while it is being wound on the tuning pin.

New piano wire is very elastic and will relax rapidly after being brought up to the correct tension. This relaxing will cause the string to go out of tune repeatedly. In order to minimize this problem, the string can be stretched mechanically after installation. This can be done with a *string stretcher*, a tool sold by technicians' supply companies, or with a block of hardwood. The stretcher is run back and forth along the length of the string while being pushed down, stretching the wire. This should not be overdone because it may adversely affect the tone quality of the string.

Once a string is stretched mechanically, it will need to be returned. It is a good idea to tune a new string several cycles per second above its correct pitch because the wire will only continue to relax and drop in pitch. The technician must make a return trip to retune the string within a few days. It may take several tunings before a new string totally stabilizes. Bass strings cannot be stretched manually because such stretching would damage the copper winding. They may require more retunings than an unwound string. By leaving the string sufficiently sharp after installation, the technician can minimize the number of trips needed for retuning. With experience, the string can be stretched and tuned so that only one extra trip will be needed. If a tuning or other repairs are to be done, the new string should be installed first so that it will have time to stretch while the technician is doing other work.

If a string has broken near the tuning pin, it can often be repaired by tying a new length of wire to the broken end by using a *tuner's knot*. The new wire should be the same size as the one it is being tied to. Figure 9-4 shows the steps in tying a tuner's knot. A bend is put behind the main part of the wire. The new wire is then flipped end over end and slid down over the old wire. When properly in place, the end of the new wire is pushed against its main length by the old wire. A loop is then put in the end of the old wire. The old wire is bent in the same direction as the new one was, but the end is put in front of its main length. The new wire is then rotated one-half turn around the old one, and its end is inserted through the loop in the old wire. This time, the new wire pushes the end of the loop of old wire against its main length. The two loops are pulled tightly together, making as compact a knot as possible. *If* the knot is not tight, it will tighten with time, after the string has been brought to

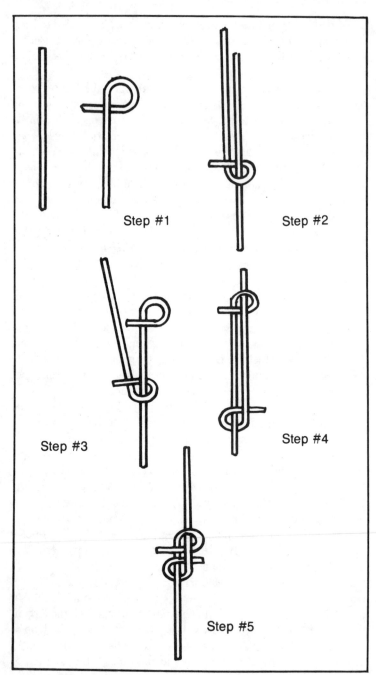

Step #1

Step #2

Step #3

Step #4

Step #5

Fig. 9-4. Tying a tuner's knot.

142

full tension, causing the pitch to drop. If the knot is tight enough when it is installed, the string will not need to be returned later because the new length of wire susceptible to stretching is so short. A knot can be made only if the string has broken above the bridge. A knot should never be made on the speaking length of the wire because it will adversely affect the sound of the string.

A treble string that has broken at one of the tuning pins can be repaired by borrowing some wire from the other tuning pin. The tuning pin on the unbroken side is backed off until there are only one and one-half to two windings of the coil instead of three. The bend where the string went around the hitch pin will have to be straightened and a new bend put in the appropriate place. After the old coil has been removed and the pin has been backed out a turn or two, the string is wound once or twice around the pin at the broken end. One or two windings on each pin should be enough to hold the string in place. This method is often quick and easy and eliminates the return trip required when retuning with a new string.

Cracked Soundboards

Cracks in soundboards are more common and of less importance than is realized by the general piano owner. The cracks are splits along the grain line, caused by extreme changes in humidity and adverse climatic conditions in general. A piano that is exposed to high humidity during the summer and then extreme dryness in winter when the household heater is turned on will often develop cracks at some point in its life. Humidity changes can be controlled so that the soundboard will not be exposed to the extreme expansion and contraction that causes the problem. Climate control systems, available through the supply companies, are installed inside the piano. The complete system has a *hygrometer,* which measures the humidity level inside the piano. If it is too dry, a humidifier is turned on automatically. If the humidity is too high, a dehumidifier, which burns out the excess moisture, is turned on.

In the event that a soundboard is already cracked, little really needs to be done by way of repairs. As long as the ribs are still tight to the soundboard and the edges of the crack are not vibrating against each other and making noise, little real harm is caused by the crack. Any change in the tone quality of the instrument would be so small as to be indistinguishable. Cracked soundboards are of much more concern to pianists, music teachers, and prospective purchasers of used pianos than they are to technicians. They are generally not a major concern unless they cause extraneous noises.

143

Replacement of a cracked soundboard requires extensive shop facilities and is a major expense. The cost involved is not warranted on uprights and most grands.

Loose Ribs

Because the ribs are curved to hold the crown in the soundboard, there is a tendency for the glue joints to fail and for the soundboard to flatten out when they fail. Loose ribs should be repaired to prevent further warping of the soundboard. The board will have to be reglued and screwed to the ribs using flathead wood screws. First, a very small hole should be drilled through the rib and soundboard to act as a reference. If the location of the plate will allow a screw to be put through the soundboard and then into the rib, a larger hole should be drilled through the board only. This hole should be the same diameter as the body of the screw. A slight countersink should be made to accept the head of the screw. The screw should then be put in place and turned down until it is tight.

If the next screw cannot be put in from the inside of the piano, a guide hole is made with a small drill. This hole should go through the rib and into the soundboard. A larger hole, the size of the screw, is then made through the rib. When making the larger hole, be sure the drill does not go into the soundboard. A thin piece of metal can be put between the rib and the soundboard to prevent this from happening. A countersink should be made in the rib this time to accept the head of the screw. A screw should be used that will go through the rib and just part way into the soundboard. As the screw is turned down, the board will be drawn toward the rib. The soundboard is very thin, so the screw should not be turned down too tightly, or the threads will strip and the board will not be drawn tightly against the rib. After all the needed screws have been installed, they should be removed and white glue worked in between the rib and the soundboard. After sufficient glue has been applied, the screws should be reset and tightened.

Loose Tuning Pins

The only sure and lasting remedy for loose tuning pins is to replace the offending pins with ones that are larger in diameter. Several temporary measures also can be taken. One way is to use a hammer and a tuning pin punch to drive the pin a little farther into the pinblock. The pin should never be driven in so far that the coil will rub against the plate. As a general rule, the coil should be no closer to the plate than the thickness of a nickel. It should be kept in mind that this is only a temporary remedy and that it may cause difficulty in tuning because of the extra downbearing of the strings against the bridge, which will add more friction.

Special bushings are made that can be inserted into the hole once the tuning pin has been removed. These bushings effectively reduce the diameter of the hole and will hold the pin tighter once it is reinserted. As an alternative, a strip of emery cloth about ¼″ wide and 1½″ long can be put into the hole once the pin has been removed. The grit side should be placed against the wood so that it will not abrade the tuning pin. This pin will also help hold the emery cloth in place. While this results in a sloppy looking repair, it can be effective. One problem with the emery cloth strip and the bushings, which have a knurled surface, is that they damage the wood of the pinblock. They are also difficult, if not impossible, to remove, once they are in place, without completely redrilling the hole.

A remedy that was quite popular earlier but that has been in question lately is called *doping*. A doping solution is made of a mixture of glycerine and alcohol. The piano is laid on its back and the solution applied around the tuning pins. The piano is left on its back for several days, giving the wood time to absorb the solution.

While this does swell the wood and make for tighter tuning pins, the mixture eventually damages the wood cells, causing the tuning pins to become so loose that the pinblock is basically ruined. The cost of replacing a pinblock is so high that few, if any, uprights are valuable enough to warrant the expense. This is true of many grands as well. Ruining a pinblock with dope eventually destroys these pianos as instruments. Doping, if done at all, should only be done on those pianos which are in such bad shape that they have only a few years of service left anyway. In the long run, it is best to avoid any piano that is in this condition.

Whichever method is used to repair loose tuning pins, remember that they will only be effective if the pins are loose because the holes are enlarged because of shrinking of the wood cells that is the result of dryness or age. If the pinblock is split or cracked, no amount of dope and no bushing or size of pin will remedy the looseness.

A note of caution about replacing tuning pins in the grand piano must be introduced. The grand piano pinblock is fastened to the piano at its ends and edges, but it has no support in the middle. When tuning pins are to be replaced, the pinblock must be supported, or the pounding needed to drive in the pin may crack it. Before pounding any pin into place, the piano's action should be removed and blocks used to support the pinblock under the area where the pin is being replaced. A scissors type of auto jack, with a wood block on top, can be used to do this. The jack can be turned up by hand until the block is firmly supported. It should not be raised too high, or its upward pressure might damage the pinblock. The pinblock of the upright piano is supported in back by the frame of the piano, so no such precaution is necessary.

Chapter 10

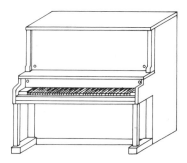

Tone Quality and
Hammer Maintenance

Many factors affect the tone quality of the piano. Many of these are controlled by the manufacturer, and the technician who encounters them later can do little to change them. An example would be the shape of the soundboard. Increasing the amount of crown changes the timbre of the instrument. Once the manufacturer has determined the amount of crown he desires, and builds it into the piano, little can be done to change it later without a major rebuilding job.

Another factor built into the piano is the striking point of the hammers. Remember that the harmonics of the piano are a result of the string vibrating in many segments at the same time. If the hammer strikes the string at the location of a *node* of one of the modes of vibration, that mode will not occur, so the harmonic that should result from it is not present. For example, consider a string that has been struck exactly at its mid-point. The second harmonic is known to result from the string's dividing and vibrating in two equal segments. Because the string must divide in two, a node for this type of vibration is located at the string's mid-point. If the hammer strikes the string there, the second harmonic will not develop. The fourth harmonic, which results from the string dividing into four segments, will also be absent. Also missing will be the eighth and any higher harmonics that have a mode of vibration with a node at the string's mid-point. Obviously, this would have a drastic effect on the timbre of the piano. A striking point that hits on a node of only one harmonic producing mode of vibration will have some effect on the tone quality, but not so drastic an effect as the previous example.

Besides quieting certain harmonics, striking point location can strengthen others. If a string is struck at the point of maximum displacement of one of the modes of vibration (i.e., at an *anti-node*), then the resulting harmonic will be more intense. The piano maker can obviously change the tone color of his instrument by changing the location of its striking point. The striking point, which is set in the factory, has been determined to be the best for a given piano, and, except in extreme cases, should not be tampered with by the technician.

Each piano maker must decide what combination of harmonics at which relative strengths he wishes to have in his instruments. Generally, in the middle of the piano the fundamental harmonic will dominate by providing more than 50 percent of the total intensity of the sound. The remaining intensity will be divided between the other harmonics. The higher harmonics tend to be quieter, but this can be affected by the location of the striking point.

In this part of the scale, the piano should produce at least 5 or 6 harmonics; as many as 10 or 12 may be present and audible to the trained ear. The number of audible harmonics will be different in other parts of the keyboard. The sound produced by the extreme bass may consist mostly of upper harmonics. The lower ones are at such a low frequency that they cannot be heard. The extreme treble, on the other hand, may have virtually no audible harmonics, with the fundamental producing the bulk of the sound.

Despite the many factors affecting tone quality, which the technician cannot control, he can have an effect on it by changing the shape of the hammer and its resiliency. To understand how this is done, it is necessary to learn how the hammer is made and how it reacts upon hitting the strings.

HAMMER CONSTRUCTION AND MECHANICS

Consider what happens to a string when it is struck by a hammer. It might seem that the string would simply vibrate with a front to back motion. The string begins to move in a spiral motion. The spiral moves outward until the maximum amplitude of the vibration is reached. After the hammer strikes, this spiraling motion of the string causes it to swing around and make contact with the hammer again. This can happen several times before the hammer can escape the range of vibration of the string. Whenever the hammer comes in contact with the string, it damps part of the harmonics that the string is producing.

The hammer, in order to produce the best tone, should theoretically strike the string at a point. The front of the hammer is rounded, however, and not a point. When the hammer hits the string, the shock is absorbed by the felt, causing it to flatten. As a result, the hammer will strike the string over an area, not at a point. The size of the area will depend upon the condition of the hammer felt and on the amount of wear on the hammer. A larger area will dampen more of the string's harmonics than a small area.

Obviously, the least amount of dampening will occur when the hammer hits the smallest area of string and when it can escape as quickly as possible the vibrations of the string. This is accomplished by creating a firm cushion under the striking surface of the hammer. This cushion absorbs the forward motion of the hammer and then rebounds to throw it away from the string. The process of creating this cushion, and thereby affecting the tone quality, is called *voicing*. Voicing consists of shaping the surface of the hammer so that it will strike the string properly. It also involves conditioning the felt under the striking surface to create the desired cushion.

The procedure for making hammers will shed some light on the difficulties that must be surpassed when voicing. The modern piano hammer is made of felt, which is produced by pressing together layers of wool. The wool fibers, which have curled ends, hook together and resist being pulled apart. Two different types of layers are used for most hammers. The inner layer is firm and hard. It is called the under-felt. The outer layer, called top-felt, is softer. To make a set of hammers, a strip of under-felt is laid on top of a strip of top-felt. A wood molding is placed along the strip (Fig. 10-1), and the felt is wrapped around the wood and glued to it. The felt is held to the wood in presses until the glue dries.

Once dried, the strip is cut apart to make the individual hammers. When this is done, the felt undergoes a release of tension where it is cut. This causes the new hammer to have a striking surface that is not flat. Instead, it has a dished look (Fig. 10-2). Remember that the hammer must strike all three strings squarely and at the same time. Because the concave shape is not conducive to this, the new hammer must be filed in order to get the right shape. The procedure for doing this will be explained later in this chapter.

Because the felt is wrapped around the molding, it is subject to large compressional forces near the wood. The outer surface of the hammer has a large amount of tension on it that is trying to pull the wool fibers apart. This surface tension is what helps the hammer rebound from the string. When the felt beneath the striking surface is being conditioned for cushion, it must be done in a way that will not destroy this surface tension. This conditioning is done by using needles to put small holes in the felt under and behind the striking

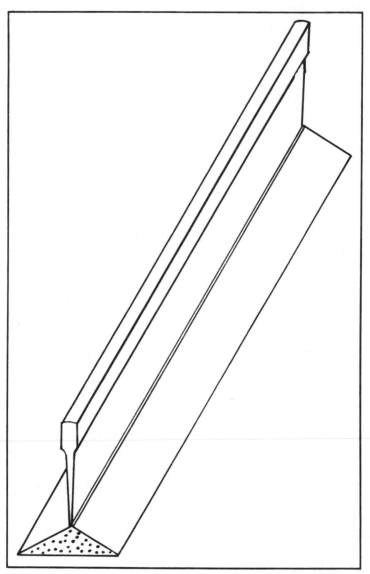

Fig. 10-1. A set of hammers being made, before gluing and cutting them apart.

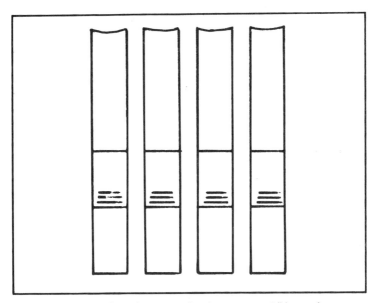

Fig. 10-2. Top view of new hammers showing concave striking surfaces.

surface. The correct procedure for doing this will also be explained later in this chapter.

Before any attempt is made at serious voicing, the piano must first be regulated. This is necessary because tone quality is dependent upon the harmonics being produced. The number and relative strengths of these harmonics is affected by the strength of the blow the hammer delivers. In order to regulate tone, each key must be played so that the hammers all strike the strings with the same force. If the action is not regulated, this is virtually impossible. It will be difficult to tell if a timbre difference is due to a hammer being too hard or to the strength of the blow with which it struck the string.

The following explanations for reconditioning old hammers and installing and conditioning new ones will cover the various aspects of voicing or tone regulating, as it is also called.

RESHAPING WORN HAMMERS

If the fronts of the hammers have been worn flat, the tone will be adversely affected, so they should be reshaped. As a hammer is used and felt is eaten away by impact with the strings, the front of the hammer becomes flat (Fig. 10-3).

If the wear is not too great, some of the felt can be filed from the

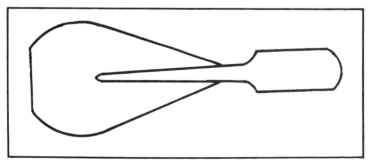

Fig. 10-3. A worn hammer.

hammer to return it to the desirable rounded shape. The hammer felt is in layers that wrap around the hammer (Fig. 10-4). The object of filing is to remove enough layers that the remaining felt has the proper shape. It is necessary to remove the action and lay it on its back so that the fronts of the hammers are point up. The filing is best done with a sandpaper stick, available from the supply companies. A length of yardstick with sandpaper glued to it can also be used. The advantage of the specially made stick is that sandpapers of different grits can be changed as needed.

To begin the process, a medium grit sandpaper, such as #80, is used. Each hammer should be filed individually, starting far down on the shoulder and working toward the crown. A few upward strokes of the sandpaper file on the back edge of the hammer (Fig. 10-5) will begin a layer of felt peeling off toward the crown.

As the filing continues, this peeling is carefully watched to make sure a uniform layer of felt is being removed. By watching the peel, it is also possible to be sure that the felt is being done square to the surface of the hammer and not tilted so that more felt is being taken off one side of the hammer than the other. This would result in a striking surface that would not hit all three strings squarely.

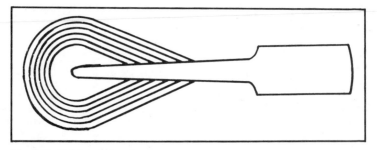

Fig. 10-4. Felt layers in a hammer.

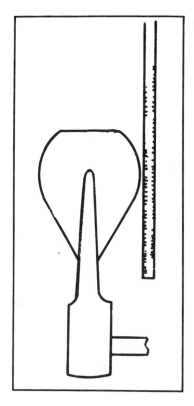

Fig. 10-5. The initial filing stroke used when reshaping hammers.

Figure 10-6 shows a group of hammers that have been filed incorrectly, so that there are uneven striking surfaces, compared with a group that has been filed properly.

As the filing continues, the layer of felt being peeled away will

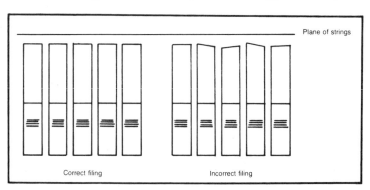

Fig. 10-6. Top view of two groups of hammers showing one that has been filed square and another filed unevenly.

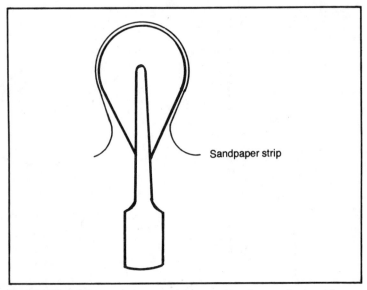

Fig. 10-7. Polishing the surface of a hammer with a fine sandpaper strip.

begin to feather out as the crown is reached. This is because the middle of the felt of the flat striking surface is on a layer under the one being peeled away. Once the crown is reached and the peeling has feathered out, filing begins far down on the front shoulder of the hammer. Again, a layer is peeled off toward the crown. Once the hammer has been filed on both shoulders there should be a small tuft of felt at the crown where the filing stopped. To remove this, a strip of finer sandpaper, such as #120 or even #180, can be pulled across the entire face of the hammer to create a smooth, rounded striking surface (Fig. 10-7).

Different grits of sandpaper should be used on different parts of the piano. The treble hammers have much less felt than the bass hammers. As a result, a finer grade of sandpaper should be used in order to file off less felt at one time in order to proceed more cautiously. Conversely, a coarser grit may be used in the bass in order to speed up the process.

REPLACING A SET OF HAMMERS

If the hammers are too badly worn, filing will not help because it would be necessary to remove too much felt. In some cases, the extreme treble hammers may be worn completely through to the wood. A new set of hammers should be installed if the old ones are

154

badly worn or if the felt has deteriorated with age and has become extremely hard or soft.

In order to have a new set of hammers made, samples will need to be taken off the piano and sent to the hammer manufacturer. The end hammers of each section should be removed. Hammers are best removed with a hammer head extracting tool. This special tool is sold by the technicians' supply companies. A clamp, which is made to be used with this tool, is placed in the shank below the hammer. The tool is then placed with its feet between the hammer and the clamp (Fig. 10-8). The hammer head is then pulled off the shank. As each hammer is removed, it should be labeled with information that

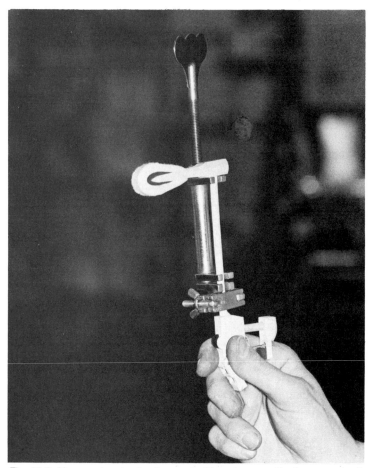

Fig. 10-8. Hammer head extractor used with a clamp on the hammer shank (photograph by Rich Strader).

will indicate its original position in the piano and with the technician's last name. The standard way to label the hammers of the three sections of a vertical piano is as follows:

No. 1, Section 1, Bass, technician's name
No. __, Section 1, Bass, technician's name
No. 1, Section 2, Tenor, technician's name
No. __, Section 2, Tenor, technician's name
No. 1, Section 3, Treble, technician's name
No. __, Section 3, Treble, technician's name

It is also a good idea to provide the hammer manufacturer with the name of the piano maker, style or model if known, and the serial number. Once the sample hammers have been removed, they should be packaged securely and shipped to the hammer manufacturer. Before shipping the sample hammers, the technician should write a letter explaining what is needed. Hammer makers may want the technician to wait for instructions before shipping them the sample hammers.

When the new hammers are received, they should be numbered immediately. It is not important where the numbers are put on the hammers because the numbers are only for purposes of arranging the hammers by size, should they get mixed up. There may be a few extra hammers for each section, so the technician must decide which to use. He should choose hammers that best match the size and shape of the originals.

The next step is to glue the new end hammers of each section in place. The striking point of the new hammers will need to be the same as the originals'. This may require cutting some of the wood off the old hammer shanks if the holes in the new hammers are not as deep as the old ones. If the new hammer sits too low, new shanks must be installed along with the new hammers. Assuming that new shanks are not necessary, every other hammer in the action should be removed. The old hammers can be removed by splitting them with side cutting pliers. To minimize the chances of splitting the old shanks, the hammers should first be split horizontally and then vertically.

After every other hammer has been removed, all the old glue is removed from the shanks. This is best done with a hammer shank reducer, which is available from the supply companies. The reducer will not only remove the glue, but can be used to shave some wood from the shanks as well. This may be necessary if the shanks are too large to fit into the holes in the new hammers. The shanks should fit so that there is enough room for the glue, but they should not be reduced to the point that the hammers are loose.

If any of the shanks are damaged, they should be replaced with new shanks that have been cut to the correct length and sized with the hammer shank reducer. In order to cut the new shank to the correct length, it is best to glue it first into the hammer butt then cut the top of the shank until the hammer fits at the proper height. The end of the shank that fits into the butt can be beveled (Fig. 10-9). The hammer shank can then be moved to the left or right so that the hammer will be properly fitted to the strings. Enough glue should be used in the butt to fill the gaps where the shank is beveled. This will hold the shank in the proper position once it dries.

By removing every other hammer, the old ones can be used as guides for determining the striking point of the new hammers. Small amounts are cut off the shanks until the new hammer is at the same level as the adjacent old ones. Once this is done, the hammers are glued in place with white glue. Glue should not be used to excess because too much will cause the hammer to sit high and will change its striking point. Excess glue that drips down into the action can cause several types of problems. Glue that falls and hardens on bridle straps or butt felts will make a clicking sound when hit by the jack. Sometimes the hammers even get glued to the hammer rail felt if excess glue is allowed to run down the shanks.

After the hammer is in place, it should be run forward to the strings to make sure it will hit them squarely. When the glue has had

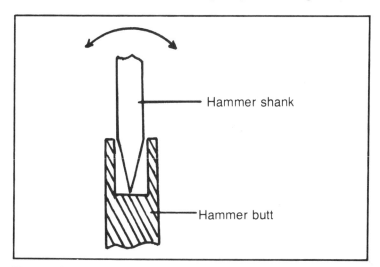

Fig. 10-9. Cross section of a hammer butt (front view) showing beveled hammer shank.

157

sufficient time to dry on the first group, the remaining old hammers are removed and the new ones installed. All the hammers should be checked for travel and alignment and the proper adjustments should be made.

New hammers will not be square across the front, but will have the concave shape shown in Fig. 10-2. They must be filed so that they will be square to the strings. Filing new hammers is basically the same as filing old ones. The only difference is that the two sides are not filed separately toward the crown. Instead, the filing begins on one shoulder and works up and over the crown and down the other side. This is done with a fairly fine sandpaper on the file. The technician must watch how the felt is peeling to be sure he keeps the file square to the face of the hammers and takes off a uniform layer.

Once the hammers have been filed so that they look flat instead of concave, each should be checked to see that it hits all three strings at the same time. Even though a hammer may appear to be square across the front, it can still strike the strings unevenly. This can be due to the strings themselves. The strings may not be level because of an improperly made plate or because of poor workmanship when the strings were installed. On old pianos, the strings may dig themselves into the capo and, as a result, may differ in height.

The evenness of the hammer strike is checked by pushing the hammer firmly against the strings, but not so much as to bury the strings in the felt. The dampers are then lifted off the strings, and each string is plucked individually. If each sounds dead, then the hammer is hitting all three at the same time. If one string makes a sound, then the hammer is hitting it later or not at all. Some of the felt will need to be removed where the hammer strikes the other two strings. Sandpaper can be glued to the side of the file and used to sand a little felt off the crown in front of each string. In this way, the hammer can be shaped so that all three strings are struck at the same time. A fine grit is used for this filing.

Because new hammers are not tone regulated by the manufacturer, it will be necessary to condition the felt under the striking surface once the new hammers are installed. This is done by changing the density of the felt to provide the proper cushion. If a hammer is too soft, the tone it produces will be soft and mellow, often to a fault. If it is too hard, the resulting sound is too brilliant, often to the point of sounding tinny.

VOICING

When a set of hammers is made, there are differences in the

hardness and density of the felt strip used. These differences result in one hammer sounding too soft, another too brilliant, and so on. The technician must play through the keyboard and locate the hammers he feels produce the best tone. This is a subjective matter, and there is no one correct way to voice the hammers. Each person will have his own concept of what a properly voiced piano should sound like. The technician must use his own judgment in finding the hammers he feels produce the most pleasant tone. His job is then to voice the remaining hammers to match the sound produced by his chosen samples.

Often, after filing, the entire set of hammers is found to be too soft. Hammers can be hardened to produce a more brilliant tone by treating the felt with a solution made of one part lacquer and eight parts acetone. Lacquer thinner can be used in place of acetone, but it dries more slowly. This solution should be used sparingly, and only on the shoulders of the hammers. An eyedropper is used to put a small drop of the lacquer mixture on each shoulder, about ½" from the crown. The hardener should never be put directly on the crown.

The object is to harden the felt behind and to the sides of the crown so that the hammer will not compress so much upon hitting the strings. The hardening solution should always be used sparingly; it is much easier to add more later if needed than to correct hammers that have become excessively hard. It takes several hours for the solution to be absorbed by the felt and to dry. If lacquer thinner is used instead of acetone, the piano should stand for 24 hours before testing the results. It is impossible to get the same amount of hardener on each hammer, and the original felt varied in density from hammer to hammer, so it is still necessary to tone regulate the instrument. Hammers that are still too soft will have to be hardened farther, and those that are too brilliant will have to be softened.

A point should be made about the hammers on new pianos that sound too soft. The first step to take when approaching a new piano that sounds soft is not to lacquer the hammers. New piano hammers have normally been lacquered in the factory. The trend lately has been to use less felt and more hardener to produce a tone that is very bright but that lacks depth and character. Adding more lacquer will only make the tone harsher. A soft sound from a new piano is often the result of the hammers' never being filed in the factory. Hammers on a new piano may have an excess of nap on their surfaces.

Before any other remedy for softness is attempted, a strip of

#220 grit sandpaper should be used (see Fig. 10-7) to remove the excess nap from the striking surface. If the hammers are still too soft and have a concave striking surface, a complete filing of the hammers may be in order. If, after proper filing, the hammers are still too soft, lacquer hardener may be used. As mentioned before, this must be used sparingly, and never on the crown.

The final step of tone regulating involves conditioning the hammer felt by using needles. Voicing tools are handles designed to hold four needles, each of which is cut so that it protrudes about ⅜" to ⅝" from the holder. Regular sewing needles, size 8, can be cut to the correct length for use in the voicing tool. Even though the tool is designed to hold four needles, it is best, in the interest of prudence, to use only one or two at a time. This will necessitate slower work, which will minimize the danger of doing too much needling.

When voicing, each key should be played with the same amount of force and listened to carefully. If the sound seems too harsh, then the felt will need to be softened with the needles. The needles are stuck into the felt, perpendicular to its surface. They are driven in toward the center of the hammer (Fig. 10-10). First, the hammer should be deep needled on the shoulders. Because the needles are driven down toward the center of the hammer, they will create a cushioning effect behind the striking surface by decreasing the density of the felt there. The needles should always be driven toward the center of the hammer. They should never be used to pick at the surface felt in order to soften it. This will only cause excessive separation of the wool fibers. It will also tend to destroy the surface tension, which is needed for a quick rebound of the hammer from the string.

Deep needling should never be done on the striking surface of the hammer. The surface tension is greatest at this point, and deep

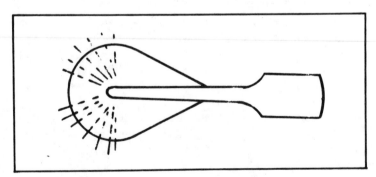

Fig. 10-10. Direction of needle strokes used when voicing.

needling here pulls apart the fibers and shortens the life of the hammer considerably.

Once all the hammers have been deep needled to soften them, shallow needling can be done over the surface of the hammer to even out the tone. As the crown is approached, the needling should get shallower; it should be avoided altogether on the striking surface.

The procedure for needling old hammers and new ones is essentially the same. Old hammers have a tendency to become very hard and may require more needling in order to be softened to the right degree. New hammers, begin softer to begin with, may need only shallow needling to even out the tone. Tone regulating should always be done slowly and deliberately. Overdoing either the hardening or softening will only mean making correction that will adversely affect the overall tone of the piano, the life of the hammers, or both.

Chapter 11

The Grand Action

The action of the grand piano is a more precise and exact mechanism than that of the vertical. The interaction of the parts is more complex, so adjustments of one part of the action tend to have a more drastic effect on the other parts. The basic operating principles are much the same, except for the inclusion of the *repetition lever*, which is what gives the grand its precise and quick feel when played. Because of the complexity of the action, and the value of grand pianos in general, the novice technician should approach grands cautiously, doing only small repairs and minor adjustments until he is thoroughly familiar with their operation. Even though he should approach grand work slowly, complete information on the operation and regulation of grand actions is presented in the belief that the largest danger is in having too little knowledge.

OPERATION OF THE GRAND ACTION

The grand action (Fig. 11-1) operates in many respects like the vertical action. Most of the parts have the same name, although they may have a different shape. There are some notable differences. The most obvious is that the hammers in the grand have a horizontal orientation. They strike the strings and are returned to their rest positions by the force of gravity. Because of this, no hammer spring is needed. Second, the dampers are not activated by the action and are not a part of it. Instead, the damper action in the grand is a separate unit, and each damper is activated by the corresponding

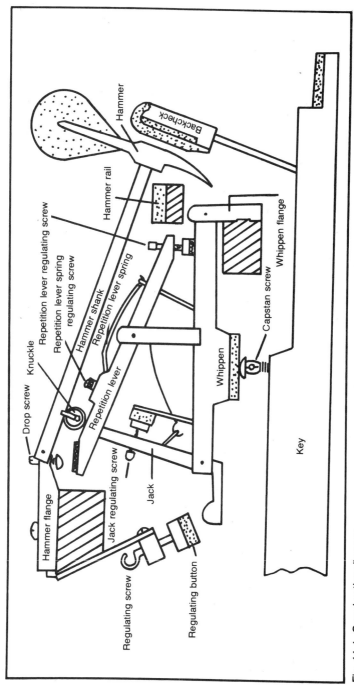

Fig. 11-1. Grand action diagram.

Labels in figure:
Hammer
Backcheck
Hammer rail
Repetition lever regulating screw
Repetition lever spring regulating screw
Hammer shank
Repetition lever spring
Knuckle
Drop screw
Repetition lever
Whippen flange
Capstan screw
Whippen
Jack
Jack regulating screw
Hammer flange
Regulating screw
Regulating button
Key

key. Again, gravity is the force that makes the dampers function, and no damper spring is required. The weight of the dampers themselves is sufficient to hold the felt against the string tightly enough to stop any sound.

The most important difference between the grand and vertical actions is the presence of the repetition lever in the grand. The repetition lever causes the grand action to function so much more efficiently and quickly than the vertical. It works by lifting the hammer up shortly after the key has been released. Because the repetition lever holds the hammer up, the jack can return to playing position without having to let up completely on the key. This is a major improvement over the vertical in which the key must be completely released before the note can be played again.

As with the vertical action, the force of the back of the key moving upward is transmitted through the capstan to the whippen. The whippen assembly of the grand consists of the jack, the repetition lever, and their associated springs and adjustment screws. The end of the jack fits through a window in the repetition lever. In the rest position, the top of the jack sits slightly below the level of the top of the repetition lever. The hammer knuckle, which has replaced the hammer butt, rests on the repetition lever, not directly on the jack.

As the whippen is lifted by the key, the jack moves up through the window and pushes on the knuckle, lifting the hammer toward the strings. The repetition lever will tend to be left behind because its window end is held aloft by a spring and has firm support. The heel of the jack will eventually hit the regulating button, pivoting the jack out from under the knuckle. The hammer is then free to travel to the strings carried only by its own momentum. The hammer rebounds off the strings and is caught by the backcheck. The backcheck catches on the tail of the hammer in the grand, so a separate backstop is not needed. When the hammer is checked, the jack has slipped off of, and is in front of, the knuckle. The knuckle is holding down the window end of the repetition lever. When the front of the key begins to rise to its rest position, the backcheck releases its hold on the tail of the hammer. As soon as this restraining force is gone, the repetition lever spring pushes the window end of the lever upward, which lifts the hammer high enough so that the jack can easily slip back underneath the knuckle. Once the jack is back in place, the note can be played again, even though the key has not fully returned to its rest position.

The efficiency of the repetition lever system is regulated by increasing or decreasing the strength of the springs and by adjusting the drop screw and repetition lever regulating screw. The spring will become stronger when its regulating screw is turned down. The reason for this is shown in Fig. 11-2, a cutaway drawing of the repetition lever.

When the screw is turned down, it pushes down on the end of the spring, giving it greater arc, and more strength. The function of the drop screw is to limit the upward motion of the repetition lever once the hammer has been released from check. If there were no drop screw, the lever would lift the hammer up until it hit the string a second time, which is what can happen if the drop screw is turned up too far. On the other hand, if it is turned down too far, the hammer will not rise high enough for the jack to slip easily back under the knuckle. The repetition regulating screw adjusts the height of the jack in the repetition lever window, by raising or lowering the window end of the lever. If it is not adjusted correctly, there will be too much lost motion, or the knuckle will sit directly on the jack. Either situation will decrease the efficiency of the action.

As was mentioned before, the damper action is a separate unit, not connected to the action. The damper mechanism sits behind the action proper. As the back of the key rises, it picks up and lifts the damper flange. This flange is connected to the damper by a wire that runs between the strings. Just below the strings is a bushed guide rail that holds the upper end of the damper wire in place. When the key is played and then released, the damper returns to the string and is held there by gravity. The damper lift rail, which is situated just behind the keyframe, lifts all the damper flanges at once when the pedal is depressed.

The left-hand pedal of the grand, as in the vertical, is the soft pedal. It works differently than in the vertical. The action, the keys, and keyframe are one unit in the piano. When the soft pedal is depressed, this entire unit is shifted to the right, so that the hammers hit only two strings of the unison instead of three. In the bass, the hammer hits one string instead of two when the soft pedal

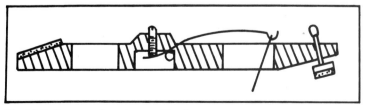

Fig. 11-2. Cross section of a repetition lever.

is depressed. The tone produced by a hammer striking two strings instead of three is not only quieter, but also has a slightly different tone quality. This pedal is better called by the name found on written music, the *una corda*. This means one string. Assuming that early pianos had two string unisons, depressing the una corda pedal would result in the hammer hitting only one string.

The middle pedal, rarely used and mysterious to many people, including some musicians, is called the *sostenuto* pedal. On the less expensive grands made today, the middle pedal is merely a sustain pedal for the bass section, which is what it does on most verticals. On the true grand piano the sostenuto pedal does much more. It acts as a sustain pedal for any keys that are being held down when the pedal is depressed. For example, if C40 and G47 are played and held down and the sostenuto pedal is then depressed, these two notes will continue to sound when the keys are released. Other keys may be played and they will not sustain, but the C and G in question will continue to do so as long as the pedal is held down. This allows the pianist to play any number of notes at once and keep them sustaining while he goes on to play any number of notes that will sound only as long as he holds their keys down. The new notes played can be made to sustain by using the normal sustain pedal. The sustain and sostenuto pedals work independently.

Figure 11-3 shows a side view of the grand damper action. Note the sostenuto tab sticking out of the front of the damper flange. The sostenuto rod shown in this diagram runs the width of the piano. When the sostenuto pedal is pressed, the rod rotates. When this happens, the flange on the rod moves upward. The sostenuto tab of any key being held down will be higher than its neighbors, which are at rest. It is high enough that the sostenuto rod flange will catch on the tabs and continue to hold the damper off the string, no matter what happens in the piano action. Any dampers that lift after the rod has been activated cannot rise above the rod flange and will simply return to rest when the key is released. Figure 11-4 shows the damper action after the sostenuto rod has been activated and another note played.

REGULATING THE GRAND ACTION

Because of the complex interactions of the parts of the grand action, adjustments made during the regulating process often alter one of the adjustments already made. Because of this, the work already done needs to be checked repeatedly when regulating. It is wise to plan to regulate the action twice in order to have a good end

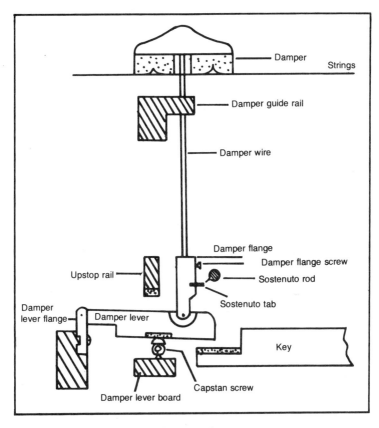

Fig. 11-3. Side view of a grand damper action.

result. Because of the grand action's complexity, and the large number of adjustments required, make a checklist to be sure that no steps are forgotten.

Bedding the Action—Preparation

The purpose of bedding the action is to reduce noises that can be caused by the keyframe hitting against the keybed when the piano is played. In order to bed the action, it will have to be removed from the piano. Once it is out of the piano, the action stack should be removed from the keyframe. The keys are then numbered and removed. Once all the keys are off the keyframe, the action stack is then put back in position on the keyframe and screwed in place. Before returning the action to the piano, the balance rail bedding screws should be backed up. These are the screws that go through

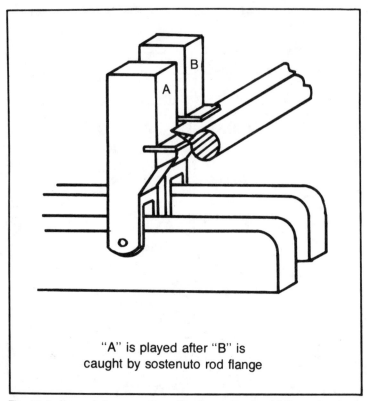

"A" is played after "B" is
caught by sostenuto rod flange

Fig. 11-4. A grand damper action after the sostenuto rod flange has been engaged and another note is played.

the balance rail and have glides on the bottom that support the keyframe on the keybed. With the balance rail bedding screws backed up, the action is returned to the piano, and the end blocks installed and secured. Be sure the action shifts freely when the soft pedal is depressed.

Bedding the Action—Back Rail

With the keyframe installed and the end blocks fastened, tap along the back rail and listen for any knocking. A knock will signify that the back rail is not sitting firmly on the keybed. Mark all areas that knock with chalk. To correct the knocking, the keyframe will have to be sanded at the places where it does not knock. Because knocking indicates a space between the rail and the keybed, sanding a little wood from the areas adjacent to the knocking should bring the frame in contact with the bed at all points.

The procedure is to put a strip of sandpaper under the back rail with the grit up. The sandpaper is then drawn out. Drawing the sandpaper out from under the frame will sand a little wood from it. The knocking should be rechecked each time the sandpaper is withdrawn. Sanding should continue at either side of the marked area until the knocking ceases. Go slowly in order to avoid creating other knocks along the back rail.

Bedding the Action—Front Rail

Again, the object is to remove any spaces between the rail and the keybed. Tap along the front rail and listen for knocks. If they occur only at the extreme ends of the rail, the keyblocks should be adjusted so that they push down on the glide pins. Recheck to see that the action still shifts freely when using the soft pedal. Check again for knocks. If knocks are found in the center of the rail, loosen the keyblocks a small amount and recheck. If the knocking disappears, the previous adjustment of the keyblocks was too much. If knocking does not cease, the offending areas should be marked with chalk, and the areas to each side sanded as was done with the back rail.

Bedding the Action—Balance Rail

The object is to eliminate space between the keybed and the balance rail bedding screws. A strip of paper, such as newspaper, is put under the bedding screws. Each screw is turned down until friction is felt when the paper is withdrawn. Once the action is properly bedded, it is removed from the piano and the stack removed.

Keys—Inspection

Before the keys are put back on the frame, the back rail cloth should be cleaned of any debris because it would affect the key height. The keys should then be put back on the frame and inspected as those in the vertical were. Specifically, they should be checked for any damage, for spacing, and for tight or loose bushing felts. After inspection and easing, the action stack is installed.

Keys—Height of Naturals

The proper height of the keys above the keybed should be ascertained, and the heights of sample keys should be set accordingly. As with the vertical piano, key height is regulated by adding or removing paper and cardboard from the felt balance rail punching. The key height is always something of a ballpark figure and may need to be adjusted to accommodate a particular case. Once sample keys have been set, the height of the rest can be adjusted to these. Feel along the tops of the keys to make sure they are even.

Keys—Height of Sharps

Sample keys are set so that their tops are ½" above the tops of the naturals. The rest of the sharps are set to the samples, using a straightedge to bridge between the reference keys.

Keys—Dip of Naturals

Dip is checked with the key dip block and adjusted by adding or removing paper punchings at the front rail. Uniform pressure on the keys must be used because greater pressures will compress the felt front rail punchings somewhat and increase the dip. As with the vertical action, the paper punchings are laid on top of the felt ones during the regulating process; they are put under the felts once the job is completed. Paper punchings are always put under the felt ones, or unwanted noises will result.

Keys—Dip of Sharps

The procedure for checking the dip of sharps is the same as above, except that a key dip block cannot be used on the sharps. They will have to be measured. When the sharps are fully depressed, their tops should be ⅛" above the tops of the naturals, provided the height of the sharps was accurately set at ½" above the naturals during the leveling process.

Align Action in Piano

The action is returned to the piano and checked to see that the hammers are striking the unisons on center. Groups of hammers are lifted to the strings by lifting up on the whippens. If the action is off-center, shims are added or removed from the action stop block (on the left-hand side of the action).

Alignment of Action Parts—Hammers

The grand hammer shanks are traveled by lifting groups of them simultaneously. A long screwdriver is slid under the shanks so that they can be lifted. Any hammer that moves to the left or right during lifting will be obvious. Traveling paper is used to correct

170

sideways movement. In the grand, the traveling paper can be used without removing the hammer flange entirely. The flange is loosened, and the end of the strip of paper slid under the side of the flange toward which the hammer moves. The flange is then retightened, and the paper strip is torn off at the flange.

The fine sandpaper, used for traveling paper, is always put grit side up under the flange. The sandpaper glue will eventually stick the sandpaper to the wood. If the sandpaper were put grit side down, the traveling paper would end up stuck to the hammer flange rail. If the flange ever needed to be changed, the paper would remain stuck to the rail, making a problem in the travel of the hammer when the new flange was installed.

Any hammers that are not striking all three strings on center will need to be aligned by loosening the flange screw, aligning, and then retightening the screw. If many of the hammers seem off-center, the end hammer of each section should be aligned and the action removed. With the action removed, the hammers are spaced evenly between the samples. The action is then put back in the piano, and the hammers are checked individually. If a hammer is off-center only slightly, it can often be moved a little without removing the action and loosening the flange screw. A screwdriver blade can be inserted between the offending flange and its neighbor. The off-center hammer can be moved by gently using the screwdriver as a lever to turn the flange slightly (Fig. 11-5). This can be done with the action in the piano.

Alignment of Action Parts—Whippens

The whippens need to be aligned so that the hammer knuckle sits directly above the repetition lever. If the lever is off to one side, the jack will hit the knuckle at a slight angle, causing a loss of power. If a whippen is sitting at an angle vertically, its flange is loosened and retightened while holding the whippen in the correct position. If a whippen is vertical, but the repetition lever is off to one side of the knuckle, the alignment is made by using traveling paper under the whippen flange.

Alignment of Action Parts—Jack

The jack must be centered so that it does not rub against either side of the repetition lever window. This is done by using a technique that puts a small bend in the center pin that hinges the jack to the whippen. A piece of metal approximately ⅝″ wide and 1/16″ thick is used to support the whippen under the jack. An angle

Fig. 11-5. A screwdriver moving grand hammers at the flange (can be done without removing the action from the piano) (photograph by Rich Strader).

bracket can be used for the support. The metal is turned so that it is on edge and supporting just one side of the whippen (Fig.11-6). It should support the side of the whippen on which the jack rubs. For example, if the jack rubs against the right side of the repetition lever, then the whippen is supported under its right side. The repetition lever is then held down, and the top of the jack is tapped very lightly with a small hammer. This will move the top of the jack away from the side of the repetition lever window.

Alignment of Action Parts—General

At this point, all the flange screws should be checked to make sure they are tight. Any loose screws should be tightened, and the alignment of the affected parts should be checked.

Alignment of Action Parts—Action Centers

The action centers are checked to make sure they move properly. They must be loose enough to move freely, but not so loose as to allow side-to-side movement of the parts. To check for tight hammer centers, a group of hammers can be lifted under their shanks with a screwdriver and then allowed to fall. Watch for any hammers that seem to fall slowly. Tight centers are remedied by using an easing solution made of 15 percent distilled water and 85

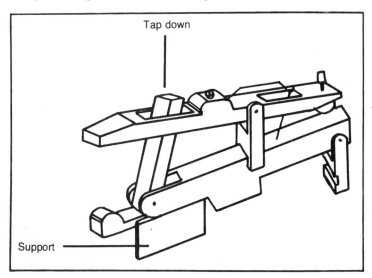

Fig. 11-6. Brace used to support one side of a whippen so that the jack center pin can be bent to adjust jack clearance with the sides of the repetition lever window (can be done without removing the whippen from the action rail).

173

percent methanol. A gallon of this solution should be made at a time with a few flakes of pure soap (not detergent) added. The soap will dissolve and act as a lubricant. If a higher percentage of water is added, more shrinking of the felt will occur.

To detect loose hammer centers, a screwdriver blade is put under the hammer shanks and then slid from side to side. Any hammer that moves with the screwdriver is too loose and will need to be repinned with a larger size of center pin. As with the upright action, a hammer should swing seven times before coming to rest. Before repinning a loose flange, check first to make sure the flange is not cracked. Any other action centers that are found to be tight or loose are treated the same ways as the hammer centers.

Repetition Lever Adjustment—Spring Tension

In order to have uniform touch throughout the piano keyboard, the repetition lever springs must all have uniform tension. When the hammer is released from checking, the repetition lever should lift firmly and quickly. The force should not be so great that the hammer bounces when the repetition lever stops against the drop screw. If the spring's tension is too great, the hammer is thrown above the lever when the latter stops moving. The hammer may continue on to strike the string. At the very least, it will fall back to the lever, sending a shudder back down through the whippen and into the key. This shudder causes a loss of touch sensation for the pianist.

To set the spring tension, the action will have to be out of the piano. The key of the note to be regulated should be struck so that the hammer moves upward and returns to check. The upward motion of the hammer must not be allowed to go unrestricted because too hard a blow will cause the hammer to travel up until its shank strikes its flange, at an angle. This can cause damage to the action center. When the key is struck, one hand should be held a few inches above the hammer. The hammer will then strike the hand and return to check.

After the hammer has been checked, the key should not be released completely, but the pressure on it should be relieved slightly until the backcheck disengages. Watch for the hammer to rise. If it does not, the spring should be strengthened by turning the adjusting screw down. If the hammer rises too rapidly, the spring tension should be decreased. After the screw has been adjusted, the repetition lever should be pushed down manually in order to be sure the spring is properly seated on the screw. If adjusting the screw does not seem to change the spring tension, the seating of the spring against the screw should be checked.

Repetition Lever Adjustment—Jack Placement Under Knuckle

The height of the jack is adjusted to remove lost motion and yet provide enough room under the knuckle for the jack to reset. The top of the jack should be 1/64″ below the top surface of the repetition lever. This can be gauged by touch. Lift the hammers up and run a finger tip along the surface of the lever. Its sharp edge should be felt above the top of the jack.

Jack height can also be checked with the hammers down by very slowly triggering the jack manually. There should be a slight dip of the hammer when the jack is tripped. The jack should also reset completely when it is slowly released. If the jack is too high, it will not reset completely. If it is too low, there will be lost motion. The height of the jack in the window is adjusted with the repetition lever regulating screw.

Hammer Regulation—Blow Distance

The distance of the hammer to the strings should be set according to the manufacturer's specification. If no specifications are available, set the blow distance at 1⅞″ with the hammers at rest. Samples have been adjusted when regulating jack placement, so the remaining hammers are set to these by raising or lowering the capstan screws. This procedure is often referred to as setting the hammer line.

Hammer Regulation—Let-Off

Let-off should be adjusted so that escapement occurs when the hammers are 1/16″ from the strings. It may be necessary to increase this distance slightly to compensate for changes that may occur because of weather or seasonal variations, but ⅛″ should be the maximum.

To set let-off, depress the key very slowly and see when escapement occurs. Adjust this by turning the let-off regulating button or dowel. If let-off is too late, the hammer will block against the strings. Let-off too early will result in a loss of power.

Hammer Regulation—Drop

The drop is set by depressing the key very slowly and watching the distance the hammer drops after escapement. The drop should be 1/16″. It is adjusted by turning the drop screw. If drop is not set correctly, the hammer may block against the string when released from checking.

Hammer Regulation—Aftertouch

Aftertouch can be defined as the distance the key travels downward after escapement. There must be enough so that escapement will happen fully. Excessive aftertouch can be damaging to the jacks because they may hit the back of the repetition lever window. This can result in damage to the *jack tender* (the heel of the jack) or the jack action center. Aftertouch should be between 1/32 and 1/16″. If the piano has been correctly regulated so far, the aftertouch should be correct. Adjustments to aftertouch are made by adding or removing punchings at the front rail

Hammer Regulation—Checking Distance

Set the end hammer of each section so that they check at ⅝″ from the strings. This adjustment is made by bending the backcheck wires. A backcheck wire should always be bent twice in order to keep the backcheck at the same angle relative to the tail of the hammer. This double bending is similar to that done in the upright so that the checking surfaces would be parallel.

Once the samples are set, the action is removed and the rest of the backchecks adjusted to them. They should first be aligned and spaced so that they are parallel to the hammer tails. Each hammer can be tested individually by checking it and comparing it to its neighbor that has had the key depressed, but is unchecked. The difference should be ½″. Remember that when checking the hammer, its upward motion must be restricted with one hand. The backcheck should be set at such an angle so that the round part of the hammer tail just clears the fattest part of the check.

Care must be taken to ensure that the tails of the hammers will not brush the backcheck on a severe blow to the key. This is tested by gently restraining the hammer with one hand while depressing the key with the other. If the check brushes the tail of the hammer, it will do the same on a hard blow to the key.

Damper Regulation—General

Remove the action and tighten all the damper lever board support block screws. The lever board's function is to raise all the dampers simultaneously when the pedal is depressed. If the support block screws are not tight, the board may rattle or squeak. The support block is often a source of squeaks in the damper action.

If squeaking, which is coming from the support blocks, does not stop when the screws are tightened, it will be necessary to lubricate the lever board pins. To do this, it is necessary to unscrew and remove the support blocks. Besides the screws, the support blocks may be held in place with glue. If this is the case, the glue bond will have to be broken before the blocks can be removed.

The left-hand block is often so close to the side of the piano that it cannot easily be removed for lubrication. If so, the lever board can be slid slowly to the right after the block on that side has been removed. If the lever board is moved too far, or too fast, its capstans may catch on the adjacent damper levers and bend the damper wires. Care must be taken not to bend the damper wires because bent wires will adversely affect the ability of the dampers to function properly. Once the lever board has been moved to the right, lubricant can be placed on the left-hand pin, and the support block on that side can be left in place. The lever board is then put back in its original position, and the right-hand block is installed after it, too, has been lubricated.

A good lubricant to use is a mixture of petroleum jelly and talc. As much talc should be mixed in as the jelly will hold. The resulting mixture is a thick lubricant that will stay where it is applied better than petroleum jelly alone, which may tend to flow.

The dampers should be tested to see that each moves freely. Lift all the dampers by pushing up on the lever board. Release the lever board and watch for any dampers that fall slowly. Mark these with chalk. The dampers can also be checked by lifting each lever singly and dropping it. Disconnect the damper wire of each offending damper and check to see that the damper flange and the damper lever flange move freely. The damper flange must have the most freedom of movement. If the centers are tight, treat them with the same solution used on the other action centers.

Insert the damper wire in the flange to see if the damper flange moves freely when the screw is loose. Incorrect alignment of the wire can cause the damper flange centers to bind. If the flanges are free enough, and the wire correctly aligned, check to see that the damper wires move freely through the guide rail. Dirt or corrosion on the wire may cause it to bind at the guide rail. The wire can be cleaned with fine steel wool, if the corrosion is not too bad; otherwise a new wire should be installed. No lubricants should be used on the guide rail.

Damper Regulation—Lift Timing

The dampers should begin to rise when the hammers are halfway to the strings. Several samples should be set to use as guides. The samples are adjusted by loosening the damper lever screws and moving the damper levers to effectively shorten or lengthen the wires. If a damper lifts too late, the wire should be lengthened. When tightening the damper flange screws, a screwdriver should not be used. Pushing in on the screws to keep the screwdriver seated may bend the damper wires. It is best to first tighten the screws by hand and then use pliers to tighten them further.

When regulating the samples, the action will need to be in the piano. The sample keys must be depressed slowly and the timing of the damper lift observed. The action is then removed so that the samples can be adjusted. It may be necessary to repeat this several times to get the samples properly regulated. The remaining dampers are then leveled to the samples so that the bottoms of the levers are all level. This should be checked with a straightedge.

Damper Regulation—Sostenuto Tabs

The sostenuto tabs must be adjusted so that they are all level vertically and are also aligned horizontally. The proper way to do the vertical alignment will depend on the design of the tabs. Horizontal alignment can be made by bending the damper wires forward and backward. Remember that the dampers must rest flat on the strings, so any bend of the wire requires a counterbend in order to keep it in the same orientation.

Damper Regulation—Sostenuto Rod

The rod flange should be 1/16″ below and behind the sostenuto tabs (Fig. 11-7). If alignment of the rod cannot be done by moving its brackets, the brackets may have to be bent until the rod is properly positioned.

Damper Regulation—Stop Lever

The stop lever stops the dampers from being thrown too high. When the keys are depressed, there should be little or no movement available to the dampers.

Trapwork Adjustment—Soft Pedal

The soft pedal should be adjusted so that there is no lost

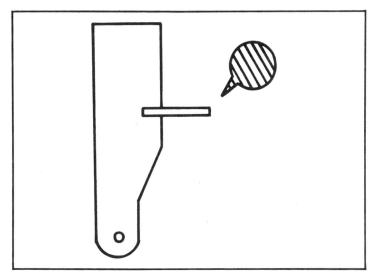

Fig. 11-7. Correct position of the sostenuto rod flange in relation to the sostenuto tabs.

motion. The pedal must shift exactly one string space on the three string unisons.

Trapwork Adjustment—Sostenuto Pedal

The trapwork should be adjusted so that the sostenuto rod will rotate far enough to catch and hold the tabs when the pedal is depressed.

Trapwork Adjustment—Damper Pedal

The damper pedal should be adjusted so that there is ⅛″ lost motion at the front of the pedal before the dampers begin to lift. The pedal should not lift the dampers so high that the sostenuto tabs cannot be engaged by the sostenuto flange.

Chapter 12

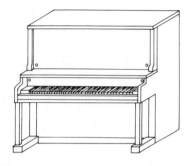

Business Considerations

At some point, the student of piano tuning will decide whether to pursue it as a hobby or as a business. Many begin with the idea that learning to tune a piano is a relatively simple task that a person can learn in a few weeks or months and use to make extra money. Perhaps this misconception comes from watching an experienced professional tuner and noting how quickly and easily he does his job. Combined with the seemingly large pay he receives for this work, the idea of acquiring tuning skills in order to earn extra money is indeed tempting.

As is often the case, the surface impression is not always accurate. As the student has surely learned by now, a good tuning is not as easy to accomplish as might be thought at first glance. The ease with which a professional does his job is what marks him as an excellent craftsman. No one can expect to read a book, or take a course, and walk out a professional. With education, one can learn to tune pianos well enough to begin to make something of a living at it. Meanwhile the tuner is polishing his skills with each tuning.

The person who is new to tuning may feel, or know, that the quality of his work is not as good as he would like. This is a problem with all dedicated, or aspiring, craftsmen. Each person has to begin sometime, and the beginner who charges a fair price for his services and strives to do better with each tuning is surely a better buy than the experienced tuner of dubious merit who has never done a good tuning and has never cared. A technician who is just beginning, but conscientiously tries to do a better job each time, will improve. A person who has his piano serviced regularly usually stays with the same tuner as long as he lives in the community.

The beginner's adequate tuning of today will become an excellent tuning in years to come. Meanwhile, the piano has been cared for by someone who was concerned with maintaining it properly. Small problems have been fixed before they could become major problems. While his first tuning may not be of the best quality, he is doing no harm to the piano and is making sure it functions properly at all times. This is certainly a better buy than the man who does a quick tuning, perhaps for a few dollars less, pockets the money and goes home without bothering or knowing how to check for problems. This individual will certainly not bother to do any minor regulation that will make the piano more enjoyable to play.

This is not to say that there is no place for the person who tunes and repairs pianos as an avocation. Many rural areas of this country do not have enough people to support a full-time piano tuner, but there are pianos in these areas that need to be serviced. Full-time tuners in nearby cities are often able to make trips to rural areas only infrequently. The man who must depend only upon piano tuning and repairing for his living may find it unprofitable to work in these areas where he must drive 20 to 30 miles between jobs. As a result, the part-time tuner in such an area should be able to build a small but consistent business. Because he does not tune as often, it may take him longer to do each tuning, but there is no reason he cannot strive for work of high quality. The part-time tuner in the city will probably be content with tuning a few pianos for himself, his friends, and, perhaps, his church.

Piano tuning is similar to piano playing in that it requires consistent practice to become, and stay, very good. The hobbyist-tuner will probably not be able to match consistently the accuracy of tuning or the efficiency in repairing as the full-time professional, but he still has a place in the world of piano tuning. Only if he pretends to be something he is not will a problem arise. A tuning that is adequate for family and friends may not be good enough for the symphony or a visiting artist, so the person who tunes as an avocation should not try to present himself as a concert tuner-technician.

JOB OUTLOOK FOR PIANO TUNERS

Luckily, the decision to become a full-time piano technician is not one that has to be made within the limits of any time considerations. A person can begin tuning pianos purely as a hobby, tuning only his own piano and those of a few friends, while charging nothing. Working on pianos for the experience alone is a good way to progress in skill. Each piano has its own characteristics, so it is important to tune as many different pianos as possible while perfecting the craft. At some point, the person who can tune and repair pianos will find himself getting more and more paying jobs. At some point, he may wish to decide whether to continue tuning only part-time or to try making a living with his skills. In order to make this decision, he must have some knowledge of the job market for piano tuners.

In general, the need for piano technicians is good. At present, more tuners seem to be leaving the profession than are being replaced. While this information is encouraging, it is not always easy to support oneself by tuning pianos as a sole source of income. Several types of job possibilities need to be considered. Some offer good stability and security. Others offer higher income potential but lack security, especially at the beginning.

The most secure types of employment involve working for a piano factory or a large piano retailer. A factory tuner works on new pianos before they are delivered to the retail stores. New pianos must be tuned many times before they are ready for delivery to the dealers. New piano wires are very elastic, causing the strings to stretch markedly after installation and tuning. This stretching causes the piano to go flat very quickly. A piano may be tuned five to eight times in the factory before it is considered ready for delivery to a retail outlet.

The factory tuner's job is specialized, requiring speed more than accuracy. His object is to tune the piano enough times so that it will stay reasonably close to the desired pitch during shipment. A good tuning would not stay during shipping, so the need for accuracy is minimal. In order to make a profit, the factory must produce as many instruments as possible on any given day, so the time required for the numerous preliminary tunings is important. Working for a factory would provide stable employment, but it would limit the tuner to the specialized skills required. Because he needs a narrower range of abilities, the pay is less than he would get if he decided to work for a store or for himself.

Large cities usually have one or more piano stores that are big enough to hire a piano technician on a salaried basis. The store technician is responsible for servicing the pianos on the showroom floor and those that are taken in on trade. The skills that are required depend to a large extent on the type of operation of the store. Some retailers have extensive shop facilities that are used to rebuild the pianos taken in on trade. They may even buy used pianos from private individuals to rebuild and resell at a profit. A technician working in this capacity would not only need to be able to tune and regulate new pianos, but would need extensive rebuilding skills.

If the store is large enough to hire several technicians, an excellent opportunity exists for the novice to learn many new skills in a much shorter period of time than he would if working independently. His primary task might be only to tune floor stock and to help the rebuilder occasionally. In this way, he can learn rebuilding while perfecting his tuning skills, all the time being paid a steady salary.

Many stores do not have such extensive rebuilding facilities, but do have a shop for general reconditioning of trade-ins. The reconditioning might include a thorough cleaning, tightening of flange screws, voicing, and any minor repairs or regulation that are needed. Any trade-in needing extensive repairs would be sold to someone who specializes in this kind of work. The technician's time is more valuable to the store when he is taking care of the new pianos, which must be readied for sale.

Dealers often have a new piano tuned after it is in the customer's home, some problems always show up after the instrument is in the home and played for a while. As a result, a store tuner may be required to work in homes from time to time. The technician must remember that he is representing the store he works for and the piano manufacturer, so he must not only be a good technician, but a good public relations man as well.

In the largest stores, with several technicians, each will tend to have one primary duty. One tunes stock, one rebuilds, and another does the in-home work. In practice, each will cross into the others' areas of responsibility periodically, so the large stores offer a good opportunity for learning. The store with one technician must have a jack-of-all-trades with skills ranging from tuning to public relations and, sometimes, even to sales. Here again, there is a good opportunity for learning, but there is more pressure because the technician does not always have a more experienced person to turn to when doing a job with which he is not totally familiar.

Working for a dealer full-time has definite advantages. The technician receives a steady, dependable salary and often has benefits such as health insurance, pension plans, and profit sharing. He will also have fairly predictable working hours, unlike the independent tuner who may work from 6:00 A.M. to 9:00 P.M. one day and from 7:00 A.M. to 10:00 A.M. the next. The salaried tuner often gets overtime pay for working evenings and weekends. The independent technician does not.

The trade-off for the store tuner is primarily in the amount of pay and the nature of the work. While a store tuner does get paid regularly, it tends to be much less than what he would make as an independent, provided he has the skills needed to build a good private business. Because so much of the work is simply tuning stock and cleaning old pianos, it can become monotonous at times. The tuner moves from piano to piano, taking breaks at specified times like any other salaried employee. Often this does not appeal to the person who wants independence, so he trades the security of salaried store work for the challenges of a private business consisting of servicing the pianos of private individuals and perhaps working on a contract basis for the smaller stores that cannot afford to hire a full-time salaried technician.

Working as a totally self-employed piano technician is certainly the most challenging and potentially the most financially rewarding way to pursue a career in piano technology. The independent piano tuner must not only be a good technician; he must be a good businessman. When working for a private customer, the independent technician receives two to three times as much for his work as he would if he were doing the same job for a store. If he is able to build a large enough business, so that he is working consistently, he will certainly make much more than he would if working for a store. There is also a certain amount of freedom about being self-employed. The independent businessman can, without reason, schedule his vacations and days off when he pleases. In the end he is his own boss and ultimately must please only himself.

The apparent freedoms of self-employment, however, are often overshadowed by the large demands upon time and energy required to keep the business operating profitably. The self-employed person can never really leave his work and go home. This is especially true of piano technicians and others in service businesses. Once at home, there will be customers to call, bookkeeping and records to be maintained, inventory to be organized and maintained, and preparations made for the next day's work. The self-employed person must also face a fluctuating and often undependable income. On the positive side, the individual who has the sort of personality that allows him to deal with these problems successfully enjoys special challenges and rewards. His success is limited largely by his own initiative and determination. He is responsible only to himself and can take pride in successes which he achieves.

SUGGESTIONS FOR BUILDING AN INDEPENDENT BUSINESS

The independent piano technician, like any other small businessman, must spend much of his time and energy promoting his business. Without promotion, a tuning business will not become large enough to support the tuner. Many technicians must work at another job and tune part-time because they are not able to find enough work tuning and repairing pianos. This can be due to having too few people in their area to support a full-time business or to having too much competition. It is more often due to a lack of managerial or business skills. Few independent tuners are so busy that they must turn down work or schedule it months in advance. Those who are have learned to be good businessmen as well as good piano technicians.

Like any other business, it takes time to build a large enough clientele to operate at a profit. When thinking of becoming a totally independent piano tuner, one should realize that success will not happen overnight. A person should be prepared to make the sacrifices necessary to start and maintain any small business. This may mean a financial investment in tools and advertising and a willingness to live on a small income while the business is still young and growing. It may also mean long and irregular hours because a piano must be tuned when the customer is at home and when it is convenient to his schedule. This time may not be convenient to the tuner's schedule.

In order to become a successful independent technician, the piano tuner must concentrate on perfecting his technical skills and his business skills. The business skills to be learned include general business practices, advertising, securing contracts, office systems, and determining rates.

General Business Practices

Creating a good impression as a professional with fair business practices is often as important as developing good technical skills. Appearance is an important factor for any businessman. A technician should project the image of a competent professional. The man who shows up clean and well dressed with a tie and possibly a sport coat will be received as a professional and will be treated accordingly. His customers will have confidence in him. As a result, they will not hesitate to call him back for future tuning and will recommend him to friends.

As a professional, the tuner should avoid making detrimental statements about another technician or about any piano or brand of pianos. There are technicians whose work is less than acceptable, but another technician should never be the one to point this out to a customer. Similarly, many pianos are of poor quality. Often, a piano owner will ask if a particular brand is a good piano. Such questions should be tactfully sidestepped. Pointing out that a certain brand is commonly a poor instrument only makes people disgruntled about pianos in general. It may also make them upset with the dealer who sold the piano (especially if they or a close friend bought it) and with the technician who brought the bad news.

Sometimes, when working on a particularly bad piano for a fussy customer, the desire to say it can be made no better because it is so poorly made is great. Even though this may be true, there is no advantage to doing so. Piano dealers and manufacturers are really in partnership with technicians, and denigrating any particular piano can only result in fewer piano sales. Fewer piano sales means less work for the technician. Poorly made pianos need to be tuned as often, or more often, as good pianos.

Even though the work may be more frustrating, the piano tuner will make just as much tuning poor quality instruments as he would working on the best. If he simply cannot stand the poorer brands, he should refuse to work on them and save himself and the customer all the frustration. A judicious excuse is better than starting to work and then maligning the instrument. For one thing, the customer may suspect "sour grapes" and feel the problem is really with the technician and not with the piano.

In any service business, promptness is important, and the piano tuner should make every effort to be on time for scheduled appointments. This is not always possible because unexpected repairs may be needed on a previous job. Whenever he is going to be late, the tuner should call his next customer to inform him of the delay. Often, when a technician is asked to do a job he knows will consist of several repairs, it is impossible to estimate the time that will be needed, especially if he has not seen the piano before. This type of job is best done in the last part of the day because it can disrupt the entire schedule or cause wasted time if done in the morning.

Whenever doing repairs, the technician must do each job thoroughly and not quit until it is done properly. At times, when the source of a problem cannot be easily found, the repairs may become tedious and frustrating. If another customer is waiting, there is a temptation to leave the present job with a repair that the technician thinks may work or probably will work.

This temptation should be avoided for two reasons. First, the customer will not think highly of the technician if he pays him to do a job and then has to call him back to do the job again. Second, even if another customer is waiting and his appointment must be postponed, it will cost the technician more in lost time to leave the repair undone, only to return again later and start all over.

No matter how tiresome, each job should be religiously followed to a satisfactory conclusion. In the long run, this will make the technician and the customer much happier. The customer who has to wait or have his appointment postponed to another day will certainly realize and appreciate the thoroughness of the person he is going to hire to fix his piano. Most customers realize these are traits worth waiting for.

Besides presenting the general demeanor of a professional, a piano technician can inspire confidence and create excellent public relations by taking the time to explain what he is doing to the piano. Most people are very curious about their pianos and how they work, but are hesitant to ask the technician questions for fear of disturbing his work. The wise technician takes time to explain in advance what work needs to be done, why it needs to be done, and how it will be done. The customer who understands how his piano works and what its needs are is less likely to balk at a needed repair because of the price. He is also more likely to keep his piano properly maintained through regular service.

If a piano tuner is to become successful in business, he must cultivate a group of regular customers. Taking time to explain what is being done shows the customer that the technician respects his intelligence and creates an air of friendship and trust. The person who likes and trusts his piano tuner will recommend him highly to friends and associates. These recommendations are the best kind of advertising for the businessman.

Advertising

Two types of advertising should be considered. One is passive, such as telephone book Yellow Pages advertising. The alternative is intrusive advertising, such as television commercials, that strives to either create a need or cause the consumer to act upon an existing need that was formerly of minor importance.

Passive advertising is of help to the business when the consumer knows what he needs and must find the person or product to fill that need. A good example is a person who is new to town. He knows his piano will need to be tuned after the move, but he does not know whom to call. He either will have to ask an acquaintance for a recommendation or will have to look for advertising to direct him to the right person. Telephone book Yellow Pages advertising is probably the best because most people will consult the phone book when looking for a new service or product.

There are three types of telephone book advertising to consider. One is simply a listing of the business name in the column under the appropriate heading. An ad, usually surrounded by a box, can also be placed in the column. A display ad, which is located out of the column and which may include a picture or drawing, is the third option. Which type of ad to have, or whether to have one at all, depends upon the piano tuner's community. The simple listing comes with the price of a business phone. Each person starting in business should check with the phone company about laws and regulations concerning a business phone. Normally, a business phone must be installed if the phone number is going to be advertised in any manner. While a business phone is an extra expense, it is a good idea to have one since the tuner is then free to advertise in any manner he chooses. The cost of the phone can be deducted as a business expense for income tax purposes.

The large display ads are most likely to catch the eye of prospective customers. They may be very helpful in communities that are growing or that have large transient populations because there are likely to be people new to town who are looking for different types of goods and services. Display ads in a smaller town with a relatively stable population might not prove to be cost effective. The Yellow Pages sales representative can help the businessman select the most helpful type of advertising.

Newspaper advertising can be considered either passive or intrusive, depending upon how it is done. A display ad that confronts the reader while he is looking at the news is intruding into his consciousness when he is not really looking for goods and services. Classifieds, however, may be considered more passive. The most effective type of newspaper advertising depends upon the size of the town and the type of newspaper. Display ads in particular, and classifieds as well, are commonly not cost effective in large daily newspapers. There is simply too much competition for the readers' attention. Display ads may, however, be very effective in small neighborhood papers or small town weekly newspapers, which tend to be more closely read. The lower cost of advertising in these smaller papers makes them a better buy in general.

When advertising in the classifieds, a tuner-technician has to decide what heading the ad should run under. An advertisement run constantly in the "Personals" listing is good passive advertising because the consumer may remember seeing the ad and look there when he wants his piano tuned. Some people read the "Personals" for enjoyment, so the ad may also serve in an intrusive manner, reminding the reader that his piano needs servicing. On the other hand, an ad under the "Musical Instruments for Sale" heading may be seen by those people who will buy a used piano, knowing it will need a tuning and possibly some repairs. The technician will have to go by his experience and intuition when deciding how to use newspaper advertising. Some experimenting may be necessary. Newspaper advertising will not normally produce immediate results, no matter how it is done. If the ads are to be effective, they should be run for a considerable length of time before they can be evaluated.

Another type of intrusive advertising, which works well in some situations, is direct mail advertising. This does have the drawback of being a hit or miss situation because many of the people who receive the advertisement will not have a piano. This aspect can be minimized by using a selective mailing list. A list of symphony contributors would probably have a larger percentage of piano owners than the general public. A piano store's list of people who have bought pianos in the past would serve as an excellent mailing list. If a technician knows that most of his business comes from a certain part of town, then the mailings can be concentrated in that area.

Each time a tuner does work for a new customer, he should ask for the names and addresses of several friends who have pianos. These names can be used to create more effective mailing lists. Direct mailings to previous tuning customers are not only beneficial, but are almost necessary if the technician is to develop strong repeat business. A filing system should be kept and a card sent every six months reminding the customer how long it has been since his piano was tuned. Suggestions for keeping such a file system will be covered later in this chapter.

The type of advertising to send is another matter to consider. Although an ad giving only the tuner's name and phone number may bring him to the attention of the piano owner, it does not give the potential customer any impetus for actually getting his piano tuned. A discount coupon may provide some incentive, but it may anger those customers who did not get one and had to pay full price. For this reason, discounts are best avoided except when starting a business. It is wiser for the more established technician to offer a token gift of a service or product with his ad. For example, he might offer a reduced price on the installation of a climate control system purchased from him. The profit made on the sale of the mechanism will help offset the loss of income from the installation, and a new customer may be gained.

The telephone can be used for intrusive advertising if it is done judiciously. Telephone soliciting has become something of a plague in modern society, and by its very nature may serve to create more animosity than business. For the piano technician, it is best to limit calls to those people who have previously been customers or who are friends of present customers. In the latter case, the tuner can call and say, "Mrs. Jones told me that you have a piano and suggested that I give you a call to see if you need any work done on it." This approach makes the call a little less of an annoyance and a little like a communication related to a mutual friend. Calls to present customers, best made a few weeks after mailing one of the six-month reminders mentioned earlier, can take the approach that the tuner is concerned about the piano's welfare. Most people will not get upset about the call if they feel the tuner is genuinely interested in them personally and in the proper care of their pianos.

Whenever telephone calls are made, the best times to call are between 1:30 P.M. and 3:30 P.M. and between 7:00 P.M. and 9:00 P.M. Calls in the morning are usually not well received by anyone, and calls which interrupt meals or their preparation will meet with minimal success because the customer is simply too busy to give the matter much thought. Similarly, calling when the children have just returned from school is also a problem because the parent will be too busy to talk. A call in the middle of the afternoon has three advantages. The children that are old enough will still be in school, the younger ones will already be taking their naps, and the mother will have time to talk and consider the matter. With so many households having two working parents, it is often necessary to call in the early evening in order to find anyone at home. These calls should not be made too late in the evening.

The use of business cards for advertising is the least expensive form of advertising. It may also be the least effective, but it is certainly worthwhile. Well-made business cards can be posted in a variety of places ranging from Laundromats to restaurants. They can often be placed on the bulletin boards of stores and shops or other small businesses that the technician patronizes. Even though this technique may not create a large return, it is definitely worth considering, especially in the area near the tuner's home. People often prefer to use a serviceman who lives in their area.

Each businessman should always carry a supply of cards to give to interested persons. The cards do not need to be filled with information about the technician's qualifications or specialties. His name, profession, address, and a phone number are all that is really needed. Often, in casual conversation, a tuner will be asked what he does for a living. Upon finding out he is talking to a piano tuner, a person may say he has a piano he has been meaning to get tuned. If the tuner does not have a card to present, the potential customer may not remember who it was he intended to call. Of course, in this situation, it is always best for the technician to get the name and phone number of the potential customer so that he can take the initiative to call later.

When considering these kinds of direct advertising, the piano technician must decide how much to spend on the advertising and where to spend it. There are no clear cut formulas for how much to spend on advertising. Some authorities indicate that small businesses should plan to spend about 10 percent of their gross income on advertising. This sort of generality is not really helpful when the tuner is deciding how much of his income to spend in the hopes of producing more income. Obviously, he will have to spend a larger percentage when he is first starting. After years in the business, word of mouth will be his best form of advertising. A tuner who is new to town will have to advertise more heavily than one who has started tuning after living there for many years and who has a network of friends and acquaintances who may need his new skills. Each person starting a new business must try different types of advertising and keep records of their effectiveness. Each new customer should be asked where he learned about the tuner he chose. By keeping good records, the tuner's advertising campaign can be evaluated and changed in order to produce more income for each dollar spent.

Besides the forms of advertising already discussed, there are also less direct ways of letting the public know about the technician's services. These generally involve becoming active in the community. The more people the tuner knows or meets, the greater the pool of prospects he will have to draw upon. Becoming involved in civic organizations such as a symphony group, the chamber of commerce, and the speakers bureau will help the public become aware of the tuner's presence.

The idea of advertising, after all, is to create public awareness of the services available. Becoming known in the community as a piano tuner increases the growth of word of mouth recommendations, always the best form of advertising. Offering to present a program about pianos and piano tuning to the schools is often well received and lets the music teachers and administrators know about the technician. Handouts, which can be given to each student, should contain the technician's name and phone number. A certain number of these handouts may find their way into homes that have a piano in need of servicing. Books about pianos and piano tuning can be donated to local libraries as another form of indirect advertising. If these have been stamped with the technician's name and phone number, a few more people will become aware of him.

Service Contracts

One of the best ways for the piano tuner to develop a steady income is to establish service contracts. These contracts specify that the technician is going to tune a certain number of pianos for a predetermined price. Because these contracts involve volume business, tunings and repair work are usually done at a discount. Schools, universities, and large churches are the most common sources of service contracts. If a church has 10 pianos to be tuned three times a year, the technician submits a bid for the total cost of all 30 tunings.

If a contract is to include minor repairs, an additional amount must be added. The amount to add will have to be judged by the technician, based on the condition of the pianos and the likelihood they will need repairs. A good rule of thumb is to add 10 percent of the total cost of the tunings. If the pianos to be maintained are mostly new and in good shape, this could be reduced because repair trips will most likely be limited to removing pencils and other objects from the action. Perhaps a few keys will need to be eased or some minor regulation will need to be done. If the pianos involved are old and have had many repairs already, the chances are good that more repairs will be needed during the period of the contract. In this case, the amount added for repairs would need to be more than 10 percent.

The means for getting service contracts is not always clear. In some communities, the public schools solicit closed bids from piano technicians who are interested in maintaining their pianos. In other towns, it is the responsibility of each music teacher to call the technician of his choice once funding has been approved. The tuner who is interested in doing work for schools should first contact the school district administration to find out what procedure is used. If the decision is left to each teacher, offering a program on pianos and piano tuning to the students is a good way for the teachers to become acquainted with the technician.

Colleges and small universities will also hire piano technicians on a contract basis. Check with the administration or the music department to determine what procedure they use when contracting for piano service.

Large, and sometimes not so large, churches often wish to have a service contract for their piano tunings. By having the contract, they can be sure of always having properly maintained instruments. It also saves them money through the volume discounts. Even though a church may never have considered a service contract, the technician who is also a bit of a salesman can get one by showing how money can be saved while keeping their pianos tuned and well maintained. Depending upon the size of the church, the tuner should talk to the minister or music director.

Contracting with Piano Dealers

Virtually every piano technician who builds a successful business does so by becoming affiliated with a piano dealer. Most retailers want to have the pianos in their showrooms tuned and in good condition at all times. Because only the largest stores have enough business to keep a piano technician busy full-time, most hire an independent tuner to take care of their needs. Unlike the schools and churches, the piano dealer does not have a contract for a specified number of tunings. Instead, the dealer works out an arrangement with the tuner whereby the tunings and repairs are done at a large discount. This is given in exchange for the volume of work to be done and for referrals to private customers. Because many people will call a dealer for a recommendation on a piano tuner, the store can provide the technician with a supply of new customers. Some stores take a fee for this referral service. Those that do not can be given a larger discount on work done for them.

The work available to tuners from dealers falls into three categories: work done in the store, work done in the home, but paid for by the store, and the private work referred to the technician by the store. When doing work that the store will pay for, the technician must adjust his charges to reflect the volume of work and the benefits of the dealer's referrals.

Work done in the store consists mostly of tuning the showroom stock. It is not expected to be of the same caliber as tunings done in homes. Pianos in stores are subject to environmental conditions that preclude keeping them accurately tuned. The store may have a wide range of temperature swings from day to night. The pianos may sit in the hot sun all day. They may get quite cold at night if the thermostat is turned down when the store is closed. The opening of the doors exposes the pianos to wind and weather. Sometimes the pianos are moved frequently, and they are certain to be pounded on by errant children and adults.

Besides these environmental conditions, the nature of new piano strings is to be unstable, especially if the piano has just come off a truck after being shipped from another part of the country. It can take several months for the instrument to fully recover after such a move. During this time, it will need to sound good enough so that it can be demonstrated to customers, even though it cannot be kept accurately tuned.

Because the technician is not expected to do a concert tuning on stock, he can take a bit less time than he normally would when doing a tuning. Because of this, and the volume of work, the tuner is usually paid 40-50 percent of his normal rate for tunings and repairs. This may seem like a very large discount, but the tuner should remember that his normal charge must provide him with enough income to cover the time and expense of driving from house to house. It also must cover the time required to explain what needs to be done to the customer's piano. In the store, the tuner can move from piano to piano and do many more tunings in a given amount of time. It is also done in an atmosphere that usually creates less stress for the tuner.

Work done in private homes for the store will be just as time consuming and stressful as any private work the technician does. As a result, he must charge more than he would for store tunings, but still give an appreciable discount to the dealer. Tuners commonly charge 50-75 percent of their normal fee when doing in-home work for the store. Most in-home work consists of tunings that the dealer gives the customer. The wise piano technician will take the time to explain to the new piano owner the necessity of proper care for the instrument. He can use the discounted work done for the dealer as an opportunity to build a business based on repeated tunings for the satisfied customers. The income generated in this way over several years more than makes up for the discount given to the piano dealer.

When a dealer refers individuals to his technician for private work, the tuner is of course able to charge his normal amount. As was already mentioned, many dealers charge the tuner a fee for the referral service. It may be as much as 20 percent. Such a fee is worthwhile because the tuner can build repeat business on these referrals. Besides the obvious advantages of regular work and the ability to build a business from new piano owners and referrals, there are certain disadvantages in working for a dealer. Some technicians feel these disadvantages are so great that they will not work for dealers at all or will do so only until they can support themselves without the dealer's contract work. There is, unfortunately, between dealers and piano technicians a certain amount of animosity, which seems largely due to a misunderstanding of each other's needs and problems.

The biggest problem facing the tuner working for a dealer arises when doing tunings on the showroom floor. The tuner gets paid by the piece so he must do a certain number of tunings each day in order to make a living. If the tuner schedules an afternoon to tune four pianos in the store, he can become very irritated if a number of potential customers come in and he is interrupted by sales demonstrations. This frustration can be reduced by assuming such a situation will happen and by saving repairs to do during these interruptions. Besides sales interruptions, customers and salesmen often do not realize the high amount of concentration required to tune a piano. They also do not realize that although the tuner is making considerable noise while setting the pins, he is actually listening to very quiet sounds. As a result, a tuner may be bothered by customers coming over to chat and inquire about the pianos or the tuning. He may also have to work while the salesman is with a potential customer.

Whereas these are real frustrations for the piano tuner, he should realize that they are part of the job, and they can be reduced. Most salesmen will do their best to respect the tuner's need for quiet if it is explained to them why it is needed. If a customer begins asking questions, it only takes a few moments to lead the conversation toward the art of tuning (this is usually what they are wanting to ask about) and how difficult it is to tune with excessive background noise. Most people will take the hint and realize that the tuner is doing a job and needs to concentrate on that job. One major problem with customers is that they often assume the tuner is getting a salary and that he will be glad to take a break from his work, they think he will get paid even if he is not working. The wise tuner, at the same time that he is explaining the need for relative quiet, explains tactfully he is an independent contractor who works by piece rate.

However, some people will not take the hint and some salesmen and customers delight in bothering someone who is trying to do a delicate job. When they happen along, the tuner simply has to take a break. People who cannot take the hint that the tuner needs quiet will move on eventually, especially if the tuner with whom he is trying to talk excuses himself and walks away to the shop area or some other place where he is not likely to be followed. Those people who enjoy bothering others will move on if they feel they are not being enough of an irritant.

Although sales demonstrations and bothersome individuals are a real problem to the tuner, he should remember that if it were not for the stores and the salesmen, he would have no pianos to tune. On those days when there is so much traffic in the store that no work can be done, the technician can go home for an afternoon off with the solace that at least a few pianos will be sold. While it may not help pay the bills this month, it is building for the future. The tuner can also reduce these frustrations by not trying to tune at a time when customer traffic is highest. If he knows that most customers arrive in the afternoon, he should plan to do his store tunings early in the day, perhaps even before the store is open. A technician can get more pianos tuned in three undisturbed hours than he can in eight hours full of interruptions.

Piano technicians often feel that dealers and salesmen are being irrational about their demands on his time. Dealers sometimes leave the impression that they want everything done yesterday. This is especially bothersome in a situation where the dealer has asked the tuner to delay work on an instrument for some reason. One morning he sells the piano and wants it tuned and serviced so that it can be delivered by the same afternoon. Even though this can be very frustrating, the technician should realize that selling pianos is not an easy job either, and sales can be lost if the piano cannot be delivered soon enough to suit the customer. Many people will decide they want a piano, and they want it today. After all, they have been thinking about it for six months (or years), and that's long enough to wait. Since the bulk of piano purchasers do not favor one brand over another, they will buy the piano that can be delivered first.

If the tuner realizes that the dealer or salesman is only trying to make a living, too, and is not trying to keep him from going to the movies with his family or from eating dinner or watching the football game, then he can put these seemingly irrational demands in perspective. At times the tuner needs to watch the football game or go to the movie or do work for his own customers. These are the times the tuner must learn to say, "I'm sorry, but no."

The tuner can also reduce this kind of problem by trying to keep all the stock in as good a shape as possible and not let it sit unattended. The technician who has, for no good reason, ignored the requests of a dealer to tune stock has no room to complain if the dealer sells a piano that needs to be tuned.

Occasionally, the demand for instant repairs will come from someone who has already received a piano and has had something go wrong with it. The customer often feels panicked that his investment of thousands of dollars is broken beyond repair, and he calls the dealer to tell him so. He may even accuse the dealer of knowingly selling a bad piano. It is in the dealer's best interests to have these problems rectified as soon as possible. Not to do so would hurt his reputation and the reputation of the manufacturer of the instrument. It should also be in the technician's best interest to attend to these problems as soon as possible because a happy customer is more apt to have his piano tuned when it is due again. The customer who feels ignored by the dealer and technician is likely to take his business elsewhere when the piano needs to be tuned later.

Another area that can cause the technician some discomfort involves a customer's expecting him to be a representative for the store and making decisions he cannot make. As far as the customer is concerned, the tuner works for the store, so he is the person to ask for the free tuning or the special favor he wants the dealer to give him. Sometimes, this is a request that the piano be voiced so that it is brighter or that it be regulated to make the touch lighter. The dealer may not be willing to pay the technician for these adjustments. He may feel that the customer bought the piano as is and that it is up to him to pay for special changes. This can put the technician in an awkward position because the customer thinks he works for the store, and yet in reality he has no authority to make such decisions.

Unless he has a standing arrangement with the dealer about such things, he should politely explain that he does not work for the store, but does their work on a contract basis and has no power to make such decisions. He should explain that he will check with the store about it and either call the customer about it or have the store call. If the technician promises to call with an answer, then he should be certain to make that call once he has the answer. If it is not a touchy situation, and the tuner is fairly certain the dealer will honor the customer's wishes, then a call can be made to the store from the customer's home. If the technician feels the answer is likely to anger the customer, it is best to talk to the dealer later and have the dealer call the customer back. This will keep the technician from having to answer for a decision he did not make.

Once the technician who is just beginning in business weighs the pros and cons of working for a dealer as a private contractor, the next problem is how to get such a position. It would seem that each dealer must already have a tuner, or he would not be able to sell his pianos. Even though this may be true, the new technician should still visit all the dealers in his vicinity and introduce himself. Although a dealer may have a tuner he uses regularly, there will be times when the regular technician is unable to do a certain job. For this reason, dealers like to keep a list of backup technicians. Because many technicians do not like working for dealers or simply become too busy, there is always a chance that the new tuner may walk into a situation where his skills are needed. If not, doing any extra work in the meantime will put the beginner in a good position when the old tuner decides to quit doing store work.

Office Systems

In order to effectively manage his service business, the piano technician must learn to set up office systems that will keep him in control of all of his activities and provide him with information he will need to make decisions about the business. These systems fall into two categories: information about customers and bookkeeping.

Because the piano tuner's success depends on his ability to attract and keep customers, he must first think about how potential customers will contact him. Obviously, the tuner cannot just sit by the phone all day and wait for calls. If someone in his family is home most of the time, then he can be sure most incoming calls will be answered. A message pad and pencil should be kept by the phone at all times so that family members can take the information the technician needs when returning the calls.

If there are likely to be many times when no one is home to answer the telephone, the tuner must consider getting a telephone answering machine or an answering service. Answering machines are effective, even though some people will not leave a message on one. Today, though, they are so common that most people who want a tuner's service will use them. The drawback to the machine is that it cannot answer questions about prices or give any other kind of information whereas a service can. The best answering machine to have is the kind that has a remote unit the technician can use to get his messages by calling home from any telephone. Incoming calls can be checked, and return calls can be made every few hours. If the tuner's answering message indicates that a call will be returned in an hour or two, the caller will be much more likely to leave his name and phone number than otherwise. Answering services, although more personal, are more expensive. Besides the fee charged by the service, the phone company usually charges an installation fee and a monthly fee. If a tuner is getting calls from many new customers each month, a service might be worthwhile because new customers are less likely to leave a message on a machine than are those people who already know the technician they are calling.

The technician should also set up a file system to keep track of customers for whom he has already tuned. He should actually have two files. One should list the customers alphabetically. The other should be a chronological file, listing each customer under the month when he had his piano tuned. The alphabetical file should be kept close to the phone so that when a customer calls, the tuner can pull his card and get any pertinent information he might want.

It makes the customer feel he is getting personal attention if the tuner knows where he lives, what kind of piano he has, and any problems he has had with it. The alphabetical file card can also have information about the customer's family, how their piano is used, and by which family members. If the tuner asks how Johnny or Christy is doing with their lessons and if they have had any more problems with the pedal squeaking, the customer will certainly feel the technician has an interest in him as a person and not just as a dollar sign. Keeping this kind of relations with customers is important to building a successful business. The alphabetical file can be a great help in keeping this sort of information handy because the tuner cannot possibly remember everything about everybody.

The chronological file is used in order to know which customers should be mailed reminder cards at the first of each month. For example, at the end of December, the tuner should pull the files of everyone who had pianos tuned in the months of July and January, since these are the intervals of six months and one year. Each of these people should be mailed a reminder card. Not everyone will have a piano tuned as often as once each year, so some people will have had their pianos tuned a year and a half ago, and some two years ago, and so on. It is important that the reminders be mailed regularly and that they be spaced at six-month intervals. Because a piano should be tuned every six months, this frequency of mailings helps to reinforce that idea. Even if a tuner knows a customer will want to wait one year or two years, a reminder should be sent every six months. This keeps the tuner's name fresh in the mind of his customer. The regular reminder will also help to deter the tendency of the customer to put off the tuning even further once the two years is up.

The reminder cards do not need to say much. They should just tell the customer how long it has been since his piano was last tuned. It should also have the name and phone number of the technician. Reminders can be made in the form of a postcard by any printing shop. Call the post office to find out the size of card that can go at the postcard rate. The reminder notice can then be printed on stock within the size limitations allowed.

When mailing the reminder cards, include a return address and have the words "address correction requested" put below it. If these words are below the return address, the post office will notify the sender of any change in address. There is a small charge, slightly more than the cost of sending a first class letter, for this service. It is worth this small cost to keep track of customers because postage is wasted and time lost if reminder cards are repeatedly sent to someone who has moved.

To be most effective, these cards should be followed up in about two weeks with a telephone call. At the very least, a call should be made to any customer who has not had a tuning in three years, in order to determine whether it is worthwhile to keep sending cards. Often, people stop playing their pianos or sell them. It is best to find this out and stop wasting time and postage on reminder cards.

These filing systems can be set up on 3″ × 5″ index cards or on standard work order forms available at an office supply store. The work order forms have the advantage of coming in triplicate, so the tuner can have one card for each of his files and a third to take with him to the job. All this is accomplished by writing the information only once. If he uses index cards, the technician must be careful to copy the information onto cards for each file. A listing in the alphabetical files will do little good in securing repeat business if there is no copy of it in the rotating chronological file.

Whatever method is decided on, the technician should take with him each day only the cards he will need for that day. He should never take the complete file because his business would be seriously hurt if it were lost or stolen. It is a good idea to have a separate card taken out to the job. If the card for either the alphabetical or chronological file is taken out of the house, there is always the chance that it will not be returned to its correct place. It will cut down on the time involved for office work if the tuner has one card to take with him to the job and two others that are put immediately in the correct files.

The technician can also set up appointments in advance. The advance appointments will require a third file. If the customer indicates that he wants his piano tuned again in six months and is well enough organized that he can pick a date and time, the tuner can simply enter this in his appointment book. Often, the customer definitely wants his piano tuned in six months, but is unable to choose a time that far in advance.

The technician can set up a file of automatic repeat customers. Two or three weeks before the tuning is due, the tuner selects a time and date. He then mails a card to the customer notifying him of it. If the time turns out to be impractical, the customer can call the technician and reschedule. If not, the tuner simply shows up at the appointed time. He might want to make a call on the morning of the appointment to verify the time. This call will reduce the chances of showing up and finding no one home. On the other hand, the call gives the customer an opportunity to change his mind at the last minute and cancel. A customer is less likely to cancel once the tuner has shown up on his doorstep. Because cancellations and postponements mean a loss of income, the tuner might want to take his chances and not make a preliminary phone call.

Besides having a filing system for customers, the small businessman needs to have a bookkeeping system to keep track of his income and expenses. The first step is setting up a business checking account. Although this may not seem necessary at first when the business is producing little income, it is still a good idea to have a business account as soon as possible. Otherwise, there is a tendency to use a personal checking account until records become so snarled that it is impossible to straighten them out. Often, money will be lost through these mix-ups.

Accurate records should be kept from the start. The independent piano tuner should become familiar with the Internal Revenue Service rules about the records that must be kept by businesses. Using these guidelines, he can set up a good system to record his income and expenses. Even if the technician does not show a profit during his first years, these records are important because his business losses can be deducted from other income earned the same year or from future years' earnings. Besides keeping records for tax purposes, the technician should keep track of his cash flow so that he can gauge where his money is going and see if it is being spent effectively.

Many good books are available to show the new businessman how to set up an accounting system. Some are available from the Small Business Administration and the U.S. Government Printing Office. These are usually free or very inexpensive. Basically, the tuner will need to give each customer a receipt when he is paid, and he will have to keep a copy for his own records. He will also need to keep statements on customers who have been billed or those who are on an open account (such as a store) to be billed later. It is easiest, though, to require payment whenever possible at the time the work is done. This way, the technician needs only to keep a copy of the receipt in order to keep track of his income.

Besides accounting for income, expenses will also have to be recorded. This means paying for all business expenses with checks from the business account whenever possible. It also means keeping all receipts. The tuner should also record the mileage driven on any vehicle used for business purposes.

Once a tuning business has started to grow appreciably, the paperwork involved becomes more complex and easier to muddle. The tuner has less time available for the bookkeeping, though, because he is out tuning most hours of the day. When a business grows to the point that bookkeeping is becoming confusing, it is wise to hire a bookkeeper to set up efficient systems and to show the tuner how to maintain them. Once they have been set up, the technician can spend a minimum of time in the office by keeping the proper information and delivering it to the bookkeeper at periodic intervals so that it can be posted and audited.

What to Charge

The reason for being in any business is to make a profit, and piano tuning is no exception. A decision must be made about how much to charge. The first step is to ask the local chapter of the Piano Technicians Guild, or several local tuners, what the prevailing rates are. The beginning technician might feel that he should charge a fee near the bottom of the current range in his community because his skills are not so finely developed. This may have some merit ethically, but it does present a problem from a business point of view. Although some customers may object to the amount charged if they feel it is too high for someone new to the business, more will object if they face consistent rate increases as the tuner improves his skill and business each year. It is better for the technician to charge rates that will stand for some time and to stick to these rates as much as possible. Charges may have to be increased to cope with inflation, but at least the technician's increases will be in line with those of his competition. His increases will not have to be larger so that he can fight inflation and try to catch up to what he feels is a more desirable rate of pay for his level of ability.

Whatever the technician decides to charge for a tuning, he should stick to that price for everyone, unless a discount is in order because of volume, such as with schools and churches. Discounts would also be acceptable to those who are in a position to refer considerable work to the tuner. For example, a teacher who gets the tuner several jobs with his students would certainly be entitled to a price break on his own tuning. Whenever discounts are given, the full price of the work done should be put on the receipt. The discount should then be noted and subtracted. This avoids the confusion and bad customer relations that might arise from one person thinking he was charged more than his teacher or church or anyone else who legitimately deserved a discount.

Once the basic charge for a tuning has been established, the rate of pay for repairs can be determined. Whenever possible, work should be charged by the job and not by the hour. Of course, to do this it will be necessary to know how long the job should take and at what hourly rate. The hourly rate for repair should be prorated against the cost of a tuning and the amount of time it takes to do that tuning. For example, if a tuning takes two hours and costs $40, then the technician should charge $20 per hour for repair work. If the job to be done is a large one that can be done in the convenience of the technician's home or shop, he may want to lower his fee rate slightly.

By estimating the time involved and knowing the hourly rate, the technician can give the customer a total cost for the job. This will minimize the possibility that a customer may complain he was charged at a higher hourly rate than another person. Estimating the time required to do a given job may be difficult for the beginning technician because it takes experience to know how long a repair will take.

When a technician makes a repair for the first time, it is likely to take him two or three times as long as it will once he is familiar with the procedure. The customer should be charged a fair rate for the length of time it should take. This means that at times the new technician must work at a lower rate of pay per hour than he would get if he were tuning. Doing these jobs for the first time is acquiring education, and he should view the lower hourly rate as the cost of his education. The customer should not have to pay for it. On the other hand, the technician should not charge so little that it becomes difficult to raise the fee to a more reasonable rate later.

If the novice technician becomes acquainted with several established technicians in his town, he can get some advice from them on how long a given job should take. When he is in the customer's home and forced to make an estimate, the novice must do the best he can and keep track of the time involved so that he can give a better estimate the next time he is asked to do the same job.

CONTINUING EDUCATION

Throughout his career, the piano technician can and should strive to better educate himself about his profession. There are several ways of doing this. Initially, he may want to attend a residence school that teaches piano technology. Several specialize in it, and many universities offer courses on the subject. This is not feasible for the person who wants to learn more about pianos while holding down a full-time job. Home study courses, if properly designed, can be as effective as residence schools if the student is highly motivated. Success is more dependent upon the student because he must to some extent instruct himself, using the written material as a guide. Because he has no instructor, he must make his own commitment of time and energy needed to learn the subject matter.

Once a technician has been practicing his craft for some time, he may want to attend one of the factory training courses. Several piano manufacturers offer training seminars to technicians. Because the aim of these courses is to acquaint the technicians with the proper maintenance of their pianos, they are often limited to those technicians who are sponsored by a dealer who sells their instruments. These seminars are excellent opportunities for furthering the technician's knowledge of pianos and their maintenance.

The most consistent and thorough continuing education can be obtained by joining the Piano Technicians Guild and participating in a local chapter. The PTG is organized to promote the highest standards among piano technicians and to promote their interests. In order to do this, the guild sponsors meetings, workshops, seminars, and conventions. It publishes a monthly technical magazine, the *Piano Technicians Journal*. It also effectively accredits technicians by registering as craftsmen those who have proven their abilities by passing rigid examinations.

Regular meetings of the PTG's local chapters contain a technical session where experienced tuner-technicians can share information with others. These meetings and the *Journal* are invaluable sources of information. Besides technical matters, information pertaining to economic and social interests is also discussed. For more information write the Piano Technicians Guild, Inc., 1515 Dexter Avenue North, 4th Floor, Seattle, Washington 98109; or call one of the local tuners listed in the Yellow Pages as a member of the PTG.

Whether the piano tuner-technician learns his craft and continues his education through books, a correspondence course, or by attending a residence school, he should take pride that he has done so through his own dedication and hard work. By maintaining a high quality of craftsmanship and ethical business practices, he can earn a place in an unusual and regarded vocation.

Appendix

Companies That
Supply Piano Technicians

American Piano Supply Company
Main Avenue and South Parkway
Clifton, NJ 07014

Ford Piano Supply Company
244 East 84th Street
New York, NY 10028

Pacific Piano Supply Company
11323 Vanowen Street
North Hollywood, CA 91609

Schaff Piano Supply Company
451 Oakwood Road
Lake Zurich, IL 60047

Tuners Supply Company
84 Wheatland Street
Somerville, MA 02145
also, 190 S. Murphy Avenue
Sunnyvale, CA 94086

Glossary

abstract—The connecting rod between the whippen and the key in a vertical piano action, also called the sticker.

action—The system of levers that causes the hammers to strike the strings as a result of the player's pushing down on the keys.

action center—The pivot point about which a lever in the action turns.

action rail—A rail made of wood or metal to which the action parts are attached.

aftertouch—The distance the key travels after escapement occurs until it hits bottom.

agraffe—A bearing device at the end of the string closest to the keyboard. It acts as a bridge for a single string or a group of unison strings.

amplitude—The maximum amount of displacement from equilibrium occurring during a period of vibration.

anti-node—The point of maximum amplitude of a wave or vibrating body.

backcheck—The part of the action that catches and holds the hammer after it has rebounded from the strings.

back rail—That part of the keyframe on which the back of the key rests.

backstop—A leather-covered protrusion from the hammer butt in the vertical action caught by the backcheck.

balance rail—The rail of the keyframe that acts as the fulcrum for the keys.

beats—The pulsations of sound resulting from two or more sound waves that are out of phase.

becket—The bend where the wire enters the tuning pin.

blow distance—The distance from the strings to the hammers when the latter are at rest.

bridge—The wedges across which the strings are stretched. They act as the fixed end point for the vibrating portion of the strings in the piano. The lower bridge is made of maple and is secured to the soundboard so that the vibrations of the strings are transmitted through it to the soundboard.

bridle strap—A cloth connecting strap between the hammer butt and whippen in the vertical action.

butt plate—A brass plate screwed to a hammer butt in the vertical action used to secure it to a flange.

capstan—The regulating screw located on the back end of the key used to adjust the lost motion between the key and the whippen.

center pin—The small brass pins that secure the various action parts to their respective flanges.

chord—A combination of several musical tones at different pitches played at the same time.

chromatic scale—A scale consisting of tones a half step apart, with 12 half steps in each octave.

clavichord—A small keyboard instrument that was a precursor to the piano. A metal knife edge on the end of the key strikes the string to produce the sound and to act as a bridge.

cps—Abbreviation for cycles per second, used to measure the frequency of a sound.

cycle—A sequence of changing states that eventually returns to its original form.

damper—That part of the action that contacts the strings and stops their vibrations once the key is released.

diatonic major scale—The fundamental scale upon which Western music is based. It consists of eight gradations of tone to the octave. A semi-tone distance falls between the third and fourth and between the seventh and eighth notes of the octave. A whole-tone distance separates all the other notes.

diatonic minor scale—A derivation of the diatonic major scale. The semi-tones fall between the second and third, and seventh and eighth notes ascending; and the fifth and sixth, and second and third notes descending.

dip—The distance the key travels from rest until it hits bottom.

direct blow action—A vertical piano action situated so that the whippens sit directly on top of the capstan at the back end of the keys.

down bearing—The downward force the strings exert on the bridges.

drop action—A vertical piano action situated so that the whippens are below the level of the keys and are connected to them by an inverted sticker.

drop screw—The small regulating screw in the grand action that limits the upward movement of the repetition lever. That movement occurs once the hammer has been released from check.

equal temperament—The accepted way of tuning keyboard instruments that modifies the diatonic scale by dividing the octave into 12 equal semi-tones. The ratio of the frequencies of any two adjacent notes will be the same, no matter where in the scale they are located.

escapement—The mechanical means or the time at which the hammer escapes from the direct influence of the key, whippen, and jack. The escapement mechanism allows the hammer to strike the strings and then rebound away from them even though the key is still held down.

false beat—A pulsating sound produced by a single string.

Fifth—A musical interval having a ratio of 2:3 between the frequencies of the two tones.

flange—A wooden support screwed to the action rails to which all the moving parts of the action are hinged.

Fourth—A musical interval having a ratio of 3:4 between the frequencies of the two tones.

frequency—The number of vibrations or oscillations that occur in a period of time. It is expressed in terms of cycles per second.

front rail—That part of the keyframe under the fronts of the keys.

front rail pin—The oval shaped pin that is driven into the front rail and is used to guide the motion of the key, keeping it limited to vertical movement. It is also called the guide pin.

fulcrum—The support upon which a lever turns when moving.

fundamental harmonic—The first harmonic of a harmonic series.

grand piano—A piano with a horizontal orientation of the strings.

guide pin—The front rail pin.

hammer—The felt mallet that strikes the strings to produce the sound of the piano.

hammer butt—The wooden block at the base of the hammer assembly. It is hinged to a flange, about which it pivots.

hammer rail—The wooden or metal rail that the hammers in the vertical piano rest upon when the key is not being played. In the grand action, the hammers do not rest upon this rail, but it stops any excessive downward movement of the hammers once the keys are played and released.

hammer spring rail—The rail to which the hammer springs are fastened.

harmonic—A part of a compound tone made up of the simple fundamental tone and a number of simple, but much quieter, auxiliary tones.

harp—The cast-iron plate that supports the stresses on the piano.

harpsichord—An early keyboard instrument, the immediate precursor to the piano. It has a plectrum at the end of its key that plucks the string.

inharmonicity—That characteristic of a musical tone whereby the harmonics are found to be at frequencies different from their theoretically assigned values. In the piano, it is due to the stiffness of the strings.

interval—The frequency distance between two tones. It is counted from the lower note to the higher one.

jack—That part of the action that is fastened to the whippen and pushes on the hammer assembly when the key is depressed.

jack tender—That part of the jack that comes in contact with the regulating button to cause escapement.

keybed—That part of the piano upon which the keyframe rests.

keyframe—The wooden frame consisting of the back rail, balance rail, and front rail upon which the keys are mounted.

key slip—That part of the piano case in front of the keys.

knuckle—That part of the grand action hammer assembly upon which the jack pushes.

laying the bearings—A term used to describe the procedure of tuning the temperament octave.

let-off—The point at which the jack slips out from under the hammer and escapement has occurred.

let-off button—The regulating button.

longitudinal vibration—That vibration in piano wire that is a result of it stretching and compressing lengthwise.

longitudinal wave—A wave form characterized by alternating compressions and rarefactions. The individual particles that form the wave move back and forth in the same direction the wave is traveling.

Major Sixth—A musical interval having a ratio of 3:5 between the frequencies of the two tones.

Major Third—A musical interval having a ratio of 4:5 between the frequencies of the two tones.

minor Third—A musical interval having a ratio of 5:6 between the frequencies of the two tones.

monochord—A single string stretched above a resonant box used to study the nature of vibrations of strings.

node—A point of zero amplitude in the vibration of a wave, piano wire, or other vibrating body.

Octave—A musical interval having a ratio of 1:2 between the frequencies of the two tones.

overtone—Those harmonics of a compound tone higher in frequency than the fundamental.

partial—A term commonly used interchangeably with the term harmonic. Partials, however, are the frequencies actually being produced by a vibrating body; harmonic refers to the frequencies assigned mathematically according to the physics of vibrating objects.

phase—Any particular point in the term of a cycle or periodic event.

pinblock—The wooden plank tuning pins are driven into. It is also called the wrestplank.

pitch—A subjective evaluation of the perception of a tone as being high or low. It arises from the frequency of the vibrations of the object producing the tone.

plate—The cast-iron support for the piano. It is also called the harp or casting.

punching—Felt or paper pads placed under the keys to regulate key height and dip.

rarefaction—The process or state of being less dense.

regulating button—A small button in the action that trips the jack, causing it to pivot out from under the hammer.

regulation—The process of adjusting the rest positions and the timing of the movements of the various parts of the action.

repetition lever—The part of the grand action that gives it its speed and efficiency. The repetition lever lifts up on the hammer as soon as it is released from check. This allows the jack to slip back under the knuckle so that the note can be played again, before the key has returned fully to its rest position.

repetition lever window—The slot in the repetition lever through which the upper end of the jack passes.

scale (in music)—A tone ladder that is a succession of tones at progressively higher or lower frequencies spaced at definite intervals.

scale design (in the piano)—The physical characteristics of the wires that comprise the different notes of the piano. It includes the diameters of the wires, their speaking lengths, and the tensions on them. It also considers the relationships of the wires to the other parts of the piano.

semi-tone—The smaller steps of the diatonic scale that have a ratio of 15:16 between the frequencies of the two tones. In equal temperament, the semi-tone has a ratio of 1:1.0594631. It is also called a half step.

side bearing—The lateral force that the strings exert on the pins of the bridge.

sostenuto pedal—The middle pedal of a grand piano that will sustain any note or group of notes provided that the keys were depressed and held down before the pedal was activated.

sound—The vibration of a solid, liquid, or gas perceived by the brain as a sensory phenomenon.

soundboard—The thin wooden diaphragm that amplifies and gives quality to the sound produced by the vibrating strings.

sound wave—A series of cyclical motions of the air molecules that transmits the vibrations of an object to the ear.

speaking length—That portion of a piano wire free to vibrate.

spoon—The part of the action located at the rear of the whippen that causes the damper to lift from the strings when the key is depressed.

sticker—The abstract.

temperament—The modifications of the frequencies of the notes of a keyboard instrument that are necessary in order to produce a scale containing acceptable intervals.

temperament octave—The first Octave tuned on the piano, during which the desired temperament is laid out for all 12 steps of the chromatic scale. The remaining notes of the piano are then tuned by intervals from these tones.

timbre—The tone quality of a sound.

transverse wave—A wave form in which the individual particles that form the wave move back and forth perpendicular to the direction in which the wave is traveling.

trapwork—The system of levers and rods that connect the pedals with the action.

tuning pin—The metal pin to which the wire is attached. Turning the tuning pin changes the tension on the wire, and, therefore, its frequency.

Unison—Two tones having the same frequency, which is to say a musical interval having the ratio of 1:1 between its frequencies.

upright piano—The tall, old vertical piano in which the action sits above the level of the keys and is connected with them by the abstract.

vertical piano—Any piano with a vertical orientation of the strings.

voicing—The process of regulating the tone of the piano by changing the density and cushioning effect of the felt behind the striking surface of the hammer.

whippen—The central part of the action that in the vertical piano supports the jack, backcheck, and spoon and that activates the hammer and damper. In the grand it supports the jack and the repetition lever and affects only the movement of the hammer.

whole-tone—The larger steps of the scale comprised of two semi-tones. In the diatonic scale, the whole-tone step will have a frequency ratio of either 8:9 or 9:10 depending upon where it is located in the scale. It is also called a full step.

wrestplank—The pinblock.

Index

215